SHOW US YOUR MERCY AND LOVE

Thirty Reflections on Life in Jesus Christ

SHOW US YOUR MERCY AND LOVE

Thirty Reflections on Life in Jesus Christ

JUSTIN RIGALI
Archbishop of St. Louis

PAULIST PRESS
NEW YORK/MAHWAH, N.J.

Book design by Theresa M. Sparacio

Cover design by Lynn Else

Library of Congress Cataloging-in-Publication Data

Rigali, Justin.
    Show us Your mercy and love : thirty reflections on life in Jesus Christ / Justin Rigali.
        p. cm.
    ISBN 0-8091-4147-7
    1. Christian life—Catholic authors. 2. God—Mercy. 3. God—Love.
I. Title
    BX2350.3 .R54 2003
    248.4'82—dc21

                                                                2002155193

Published by Paulist Press
997 Macarthur Boulevard
Mahwah, New Jersey 07430

www.paulistpress.com

Printed and bound in the
United States of America

Dedication

TO HIS HOLINESS POPE JOHN PAUL II
as he tirelessly proclaims
Jesus Christ
"the Way and the Truth and the Life."

Table of Contents

Introduction

Show Us Your Mercy and Love presents thirty reflections on life in Jesus Christ. These reflections treat major aspects of Christian discipleship, emphasizing in a special way *divine mercy*, which His Holiness Pope John Paul 11 calls "God's greatest attribute."

The aim of the book is to concentrate the reader's attention on the person of Jesus Christ, source of life and holiness for all. It wishes to proclaim the love of God that passes through the heart of Jesus Christ and in the face of our sinfulness and need reveals itself as mercy.

Originally, these reflections were offered in the form of an extended retreat given to consecrated Religious. The presentation has been modified to apply more relevantly to all the members of the church, while still retaining specific elements of consecrated life, such as the evangelical counsels of chastity, poverty and obedience.

This collection of spiritual reflections invites the reader to a total acceptance of Jesus in faith and to the manifestation of acceptance in trust.

To accept Jesus totally is to accept his church, his sacraments, his way of life, his commandment of love. It means accepting his mission of evangelization in this new millennium, which is so important in the history of the gospel.

To accept Jesus is to accept him in his divinity and his humanity, to confess him—in the words of Pope Leo the Great—"consubstantial with His Father and consubstantial with His Mother." To accept Jesus is to be loved by his Father and to be filled with his Spirit.

May these pages serve the cause of Christ's kingdom and help show his mercy and love.

1. Jesus

"Why Are You Here?"

In the First Book of Kings we read about how the prophet Elijah experiences grave difficulties in his mission (cf. 1 Kgs 19). Elijah flees from Jezebel, the wicked wife of the wicked king Ahab. The prophet is profoundly discouraged and prays for death.

God intervenes and sends his angel to give Elijah food to prepare him for a journey to the mountain of God, Horeb. It took forty days for him to make the journey.

Elijah came to a cave and took shelter. And the Lord spoke to Elijah and told him to go outside and await his coming. He said: "The Lord will be passing by."

First came a strong and heavy wind that was rending the mountains and crushing the rocks. The Lord's promise was not yet fulfilled, because he was not in the wind. Then came an earthquake, but the Lord was not in the earthquake. After the earthquake there was fire, but the Lord was not in the fire.

After the fire there was a tiny whispering sound. And from this environment of peace God spoke to him, posing a tremendous question: "Elijah, why are you here?" Elijah tried to explain that his life was in danger because of his fidelity and his zeal.

God then told him to move on. A mission awaited Elijah. He had to anoint the king of Israel; he had to anoint the prophet Elisha to succeed himself. There was much for Elijah to do, but God was with him.

The question God addressed to Elijah, he addresses to us: "Why are you here?"

Listening to God is a wonderful opportunity for us to realize why we are here, to restate our purpose in life. We have the opportunity to answer God, evoking his love, which is the explanation of our lives, the explanation of our Christian vocation. Does not the love of God that passes through the sacred heart of Jesus explain so much to us?

God's question to Elijah becomes Jesus' question to us: "Why are you here?" He deserves an answer in a *dialogue of love*. Are we not called to reflect on why we are here? A dialogue of love is necessary so that our ideas may be clarified and our intentions purified. Jesus desires intimacy with us; we need intimacy with him.

Jesus knows the answer to the question he asks us: "Why are you here?" But *he wants us to tell him*, over and over again. He wants us to understand and express better our relationship with him in Christian living and in our vocation in life—all of which presupposes his heart as a burning furnace of charity.

The opportunity is before us to explore intimacy with Christ, enter more deeply into his heart. We have to do this in order to find joy and strength for our journey. The journey is long, but exhilarating and fulfilling. Let us remember the question: "Why are you here?"

Concentration on Jesus

I remember taking part years ago in a big ceremony in the Vatican in honor of Mother Teresa of Calcutta. She had just received an international award. The Holy See wanted to highlight her accomplishments in the presence of the International Diplomatic Corps. The Holy Father was presiding.

Before the ceremony began, I spoke to Mother Teresa about her speech and I asked her: "Mother Teresa, what will you be speaking about today?" She answered me with a smile, saying simply: "I don't know. All I know is that I will be talking about Jesus."

This is my personal goal as a priest and a bishop: to talk about Jesus: to proclaim his divinity and his humanity; to speak about his way of life, about his love for us, the mission that he has entrusted to us through his church; to speak about the fulfillment and the joy we receive in knowing him, loving him and serving him and all those who share humanity with him, especially those in need.

Our concentration must always be on Jesus and not on ourselves. We must concentrate on his love and his word and the challenges that he offers us. Our encounter with Jesus is a personal encounter with him as he lives in the communion of the Most Blessed Trinity.

One aspect of this encounter that is important is *the personal encounter with Jesus in the sacrament of penance.* It is his right to encounter us; it is our right to encounter him. On our part it is an encounter of faith and trust, in which we acknowledge not only Jesus, but also his sacramental plan that is realized through his humanity and the humanity of the priest who represents him. Confession is a special time to say to Jesus: *Jesus, I trust in you!*

On the part of Jesus it is an encounter of love, in which he infuses into your heart the pardon that comes forth from the ocean of mercy that has its origin in his Father. *To encounter Jesus is to know his Father and his Father's mercy.*

Today God has a message for us—a wonderful message, the message he gave to Elijah. He is saying: "The Lord will be passing by."

We must experience and explore the presence of God in the heart of Jesus and then answer his question: "Why are you here?" We know the answer, but we have to tell it to God!

As for me, I am here to talk about Jesus! The following chapters are meant to show this.

2. The Story of God's Love

When the Holy Father came to the United States on one of his pastoral visits, he stated that he had come in order to tell again *the story of God's love.*

Our whole life is explained by God's love. Everything we do has value only to the extent that it helps us and others to share in God's love. The story of God's love goes back to the *communion of the Most Blessed Trinity,* which exists from all eternity. In God, love and life are identical. Only by God's revelation can we know about God's life and God's love.

In the New Testament we have this wonderful revelation. Jesus came on earth to enable us to know about eternal life. Jesus himself said: "This is eternal life that they should know you, the only true God and the one whom you sent, Jesus Christ" (John 17:3). But Jesus also explained to us how through him we share in God's life. He told us: "I am the way and the truth and the life" (John 14:6).

But *why* is Jesus the way and the truth and the life? He is the way and the truth and the life for us, *because he is the son of the Eternal Father.* From all eternity God is a Father. His Son is called the Eternal Word of God. In the creed of the church we proclaim that the Son is "begotten, not made."

We would never have known about this Father and Son relationship, had Jesus not revealed it to us. Jesus, in effect, tells us that he and the Father are one—one in divinity, one in the divine nature. He is, in the words of the creed: consubstantial with his Father; he is one in being with his Father.

A Communion of Love

But Jesus also reveals to us that he and his Father live *in the communion of three persons.* The story of God's love begins here. Jesus tells us that *the Father loves him* and that *he loves the Father.* This is the greatest revelation of God, because it is the explanation of his own trinitarian life of love and the explanation of his love for the world.

The love of the Father for the Son and the love of the Son for the Father are so real and so personal that it is another person: the third person of the Most Blessed Trinity, whom we call the Holy Spirit. *The Holy Spirit brings to completion the life of God.* He is the term of the divine operations in the Trinity. The Holy Spirit personalizes and personifies the love of the Father and the Son. He is the Spirit of the Father and the Son. He is the Spirit of their love.

Jesus taught us all about God's love and then sent the Spirit of love into the church to make it possible for us to hand down this teaching, to explain it and to understand its importance—even if we can never grasp it completely.

God Sends His Son

The story of God's love does not stop in the Most Blessed Trinity. It could have, but God chose to share his love with us. And so Jesus tells us: "For God so loved the world that he gave his only Son, so that everyone who believes in him might not perish but might have eternal life. For God did not send his Son into the world to condemn the world, but that the world might be saved through him" (John 3:16–17).

The continuing story of God's love is expressed so well in these two words: God *gave* his Son, God *sent* his Son!

We all know how this took place: how the Angel Gabriel announced to Mary that she was to be the Mother of God, how Mary consented and how God's Eternal Word, his Eternal Son, took on our flesh in the womb of the Virgin Mary and became man.

The second person of the Most Blessed Trinity who from all eternity is "consubstantial with His Father," now became "consubstantial with His Mother." In the incarnation Jesus presents himself to the world as true God and true Man. The Son who is loved by his Father comes to earth to take on our human nature, in order to reveal to us the love of God and through his death and resurrection *to enable us to share God's love* and *to respond to it*.

How beautiful the story of God's love! How wonderful God's plan for us!

Despite the fact that God has but one Eternal Son, it is the Father's plan, in and through Christ, to adopt us as his children, to make us by grace his sons and daughters in such a way that Christ, who is the only-begotten Son becomes the firstborn in a family of many (cf. Rom 8:29). God wills that all those who are adopted as his sons and daughters be *conformed to the image of his one Son*. We are therefore, in the expression of the church: *sons and daughters in the Son (filii in Filio)*. As brothers and sisters of Christ, as sons and daughters of the Eternal Father, our greatest dignity is to be conformed to Jesus to the extent that the Father, looking on us, calls us "Jesus," and Jesus, looking on us, calls us "me." "As long as you did it to the least of my brothers, you did it to me." What an incredible chapter of the story of God's love: by grace we are not only sons and daughters of God but by grace we are identified with the Son of God. In us the Father sees and loves his only Son!

Response to God's Love

Where does all this lead us? It leads us to the challenge of a response—*a response to God's love*.

As God's children, conformed to the image of his one Son, we must love like the Son. We must love the Father in a way that is worthy of Jesus, who is the Son. Our love must be total, sacrificial and joyful. It is forever!

There is another aspect to the story of God's love; it is *our love for one another*. Saint John spells it out for us when he says: "Beloved, if God so loved us, we also must love one another. . . . if we love one another,

God remains in us, and his love is brought to perfection in us" (1 John 4:11–12).

The story of God's love becomes a *challenge for the church* and all her members. It is the challenge for everyone to practice justice and truth, chastity and charity, without which God's love is not embraced or responded to. It is the challenge for everyone of humble Christian service. The story of God's love, signified in the heart of Christ, becomes a special challenge for each of us in our vocation and mission of service to the church.

The Spirit of God's love, who dwells in the Most Blessed Trinity and in whom the Father and the Son love each other, is the Spirit who conforms us to Jesus. And it is Jesus, acting in the Holy Spirit, who enables us to love one another as he has loved us.

How powerful this Jesus! How worthy this faithful witness of God's love! How deserving of our trust! Let us say to him: *Jesus, I trust in you!*

3. Conversion

Something that is very important in your life and in mine is conversion—conversion to God.

Saint John gives us these beautiful words: "But if we walk in the light as he is in the light, then we have fellowship with one another, and the blood of his Son Jesus cleanses us from all sin. If we say, 'We are without sin,' we deceive ourselves, and the truth is not in us. If we acknowledge our sins, he is faithful and just and will forgive our sins and cleanse us from every wrongdoing. If we say, 'We have not sinned,' we make him a liar, and his word is not in us" (1 John 1:7–10).

As we reflect on this important topic of conversion, we are struck especially by St. John's words that the blood of Jesus cleanses us from all sin. We must never allow ourselves to concentrate on ourselves or on our sins; we must concentrate only on *the invitation of Jesus to conversion* and on *the efficacy of his precious blood.*

The gospel opens with the invitation of Jesus to recognize our sins, to repent and to be converted. What are the first words of Jesus in his public life as he appears on the scene of salvation history? Saint Mark records these words for us: "This is the time of fulfillment. The kingdom of God is at hand. Repent, and believe in the gospel" (Mark 1:15). With these words Jesus introduces his message about the kingdom of God. With these words he launches the invitation to all generations of people *to turn to God*, to be converted and to find life and salvation in his precious blood.

John the Baptist had prepared the way for Jesus. John the Baptist had already said: "Repent, for the kingdom of heaven is at hand!" (Matt 3:2). The announcement of John the Baptist shows how authentic his preparation for Christ was, how genuine a precursor he was to prepare the way for Jesus, who would preach conversion.

"What Are We to Do?"

From the very beginning the church has understood the call of Jesus to conversion, and throughout the centuries this call has been reiterated. Saint Peter, on the day of Pentecost, responded to the question of the people of the house of Israel who asked: "What are we to do?" His response was: "Repent and be baptized, every one of you, in the name of Jesus Christ for the forgiveness of your sins; and you will receive the gift of the holy Spirit" (Acts 2:37–38).

Later on we find St. Paul also proclaiming the need for conversion. He speaks to King Agrippa saying: "I preached the need to repent and turn to God, and to do works giving evidence of repentance" (Acts 26:20). He also adds that this message of conversion that he preached so faithfully in obedience to

11

the teachings of Jesus was the reason why he was seized in the temple and why the crowd tried to kill him.

What is even of greater importance is that the baptism of Jesus took place in the total context of the preaching of John the Baptist about repentance and conversion, which involved the testimony of God the Father. Only three times in the history of the world, as we find in the gospels, has the voice of the Eternal Father been heard. Saint Luke presents to us one of these magnificent occasions. It is the baptism of Jesus. The voice of the Eternal Father came from Heaven: "You are my beloved Son; with you I am well pleased" (Luke 3:22). With these words not only does he present his Son to the world, but the Eternal Father also ratifies the preaching of John the Baptist, who is the precursor of Jesus precisely in his proclamation of the message of conversion.

What does conversion mean? What Jesus is asking us is to recognize sin in our lives. He is asking us to recognize God's commandments; to recognize the need to respond to God's love, the need to live in the style of the Beatitudes. Conversion goes further than this. It is also *a call to recognize the power of God's grace*, to recognize that the forgiveness of sins is greater than sin itself.

Saint Paul tells us: "where sin increased, grace overflowed all the more" (Rom 5:20). What is so comforting in the message of Jesus is that, as he calls us to conversion, he assures us of *the mercy of his Father*. And on the first Easter evening Jesus will give forever to his church the sacrament of penance, the great means whereby everyone who embraces him can be reconciled to God.

We ask ourselves: *Why is conversion so important?* Why did it constitute the message of John the Baptist? Why was it the first announcement of Jesus? Why has the church picked up this proclamation with such insistence?

We know that God is calling us to be like himself. He is inviting us to remove the obstacles that impede our likeness to him and our configuration to his Son. In the Book of Leviticus we read these solemn words of God: "Since I, the LORD, brought you up from the land of Egypt that I might be your God, you shall be holy, because I am holy" (Lev 11:45).

Later on in the gospel Jesus will completely ratify this injunction. He will say: "So be perfect, just as your heavenly Father is perfect" (Matt 5:48). *To be holy is our vocation.* To be holy corresponds to God's will in creating us. To be holy corresponds to the truth of our nature. By calling us to conversion, Christ is telling us that there is another opportunity to turn to God, to divest ourselves of sin and to live according to the holiness of God. Yes, all this is possible. Saint John tells us: "I am writing this to you so that you may not commit sin. But if anyone does sin, we have an Advocate with the Father, Jesus Christ the righteous one. He is expiation for our sins, and not for our sins only but for those of the whole world" (1 John 2:1–2).

Sin's Impact on Christ

To understand the priority that Christ and his Father attach to our conversion we must understand also *the effect that sin has had on Christ.* There are two more texts of sacred scripture that we must reflect on.

The prophet Isaiah already foretold *the effects of our sins on Christ.* Let us listen to the prophet: "Yet it was our infirmities that he bore, / our sufferings that he endured, / While we thought of him as stricken, / as one smitten by God and afflicted. / But he was pierced for our offenses, / crushed for our sins, / Upon him was the chastisement that makes us whole, / by his stripes we were healed. / We had all gone astray like sheep, / each following his own way; / But the LORD laid upon him / the guilt of us all. / Though he was harshly treated, he submitted / and opened not his mouth; / Like a lamb led to the slaughter / or a sheep before the shearers, / he was silent and opened not his mouth. / Oppressed and condemned, he was taken away, / and who would have thought any more of his destiny?" (Isa 53:4–8).

The impact that sin has had on Christ is indeed a most important reason for our conversion. Conversion involves the renunciation of the terrible evil that has struck Christ in such a personal way. The renunciation of this evil is necessary for reconciliation with God and the church. Saint Paul in his Second Letter to the Corinthians presents to us a text that we can never sufficiently fathom. He describes to us, in terms that only he as an apostle could be authorized to use, *the enormity of sin.* He tells us first: "So we are ambassadors for Christ, as if God were appealing through us. We implore you on behalf of Christ, to be reconciled to God." But then he goes on immediately to add this phrase, which we must repeatedly reflect on: "For our sake he made him to be sin who did not know sin, so that we might become the righteousness of God in him" (2 Cor 5:20–21).

This text is very important for our total understanding of sin, conversion and holiness. In the invitation to conversion, what is it that Jesus is asking us to renounce? Jesus is asking us to renounce what St. Paul has just told us has turned him, Jesus, into sin! The explanation is so graphic. Not only is Christ presented as being struck by sin, as suffering for our sins, but he is presented by St. Paul *as becoming sin*. This gives us some inkling of what sin means for Jesus. Jesus knows the repugnance of his Father for sin. Jesus knows that he is the Father's beloved Son. Jesus knows that his relationship to the Father and the Father's relationship to him is the relationship of love in the Holy Spirit. And yet Jesus, in the expression of St. Paul, looks upon himself *as being sin*, as being transformed into sin by the sin committed by his brothers and sisters. Becoming sin in this terrible sense, Jesus realizes the repugnance that his Father has for sin, and this becomes for him an immense suffering.

All of this was part of his passion and death. All of this was done in order that we might be saved. There is no way that we can fail to recognize the tremendous chastisement that Jesus has taken upon himself in permitting himself "to become sin" for our sake.

15

"That We Might Become the Holiness of God."

Finally, it is necessary for us to see all this within the magnificence of God's plan. It is all spelled out in God's holy word. Terrible and excruciating as this pain was for Christ to become sin, to be viewed as sin by his sinless and loving Father—terrible as this is—we see in this text from St. Paul the reason why Christ did this. Saint Paul concludes his statement by saying: "...so that we might become the righteousness of God in him."

In all the scriptures there is no more dramatic presentation of sin than this. There is nothing that shows the contrast between holiness and sin more than this; there is nothing that shows more than this *how much Christ suffered to make us holy and to bring us to conversion.* And so Christ becomes sin for us that we might become the righteousness of God, or, in other words, the justice of God, the holiness of God. Christ becomes sin that we might become the holiness of God!

What is being asked of us? That with God's grace, through the power of the love with which Christ undertook his passion and death, we exercise our freedom and turn to God to renounce sin, so that we may indeed be the holiness of God!

What is being asked of us? That we turn with trust to Jesus, who "became sin" for us and who is the cause of our holiness, and say to him: *Jesus, I trust in you!*

4. *Surrender and Service*

The Gospel of St. John speaks to us about *important elements in the Christian life*: the grain of wheat that falls and dies, and the fruit that is produced thereby (cf. John 12:24–26).

We have a beautiful example in Deacon Lawrence, incredibly honored in the early church, who gave himself, in life and in death, for the church. The gift of his life of service was blessed with fruitfulness. He is a great example, by *his joy and his humor*, of what St. Paul calls: "a cheerful giver."

Is this not a special charism: cheerful giving—to respond to the living presence of Jesus in the depth of our being? A beautiful form of surrender and fruitful service is found in daily prayer and sacrifice. Its fruit is joyful, cheerful giving! Where there is surrender, where there is "cheerful giving" there is fruitfulness. Saint Lawrence proves it.

There is a close relationship between surrender and service. Surrender to God makes service to one's neighbor possible, and guarantees its effectiveness, its fruitfulness. But surrender does something else. *Surrender guarantees the supreme reward of service.*

In the gospel, Jesus speaks of service in terms of the Trinity. He brings his Father into the picture. He speaks of the Father as honoring those who serve him. Do we really grasp *the importance that Jesus is attaching to service*—whether it be the service rendered by St. Lawrence or by us?

Jesus himself is the Word of the Father. His identity, beautifully explained in the language of theology, is *Totus ad Patrem* (the one whose existence is totally directed to the Father). In extolling the value of service rendered to him, Jesus involves his Father. He promises that his Father will honor those who serve him. There is *nothing greater that Jesus can promise; there is nothing greater that we can receive than to be honored by his Father.*

Our life like that of St. Lawrence, *our surrender* like the grain of wheat that falls to the earth and dies, and *our daily service are what Jesus is talking about:* "Anyone who serves me, the Father will honor." Do we believe this? Do we trust? Yes. *Jesus, I trust in you!*

A Price for Fruitfulness

Saint Clare, coming ten centuries after Lawrence, still speaks eloquently to us about surrender. We honor her as a virgin, a Religious, a foundress, a prophetic figure in contemplation and intercession for the church.

Clare holds the title of her charisms delicately, as does Ezekiel the prophet: Both he and she knew that charisms are gratuitous gifts of God. *The prophet is nothing without God.* The charism of Ezekiel was *to eat the word of God, then go and speak it.* Clare's charism was to be *a joyful example in the living of the word:* How sweet to my taste is your promise! (cf. Ps 119:103).

She found light and joy in the word of God, in his promises.

Certainly Clare lived in the childlike simplicity and innocence that Jesus proposes to us in the gospel: "Amen, I say to you, unless you turn and become like children, you will not enter the kingdom of heaven" (Matt 18:3).

Clare's surrender made possible the full efficacy of her charisms. *Her legacy to the church* of prayer, intercession and the drawing down of mercy on God's people *is related to her personal fidelity and holiness*—her surrender to Christ Jesus. For works of such importance, God only chooses those who will surrender themselves completely to him in fidelity and love.

In the gospel Jesus alludes to his mission of mercy. He is the one who, as the good shepherd, leaves the ninety-nine to go after the one stray sheep. He does not want a single one ever to be lost—so merciful is he!

In the mystery of the church we know that Christ shares his work of mercy and salvation with us. But there is *a price for fruitfulness*, for supernatural effectiveness—*a price to pay for the triumph of God's mercy*, for the conversion of the world, for the spread of the gospel. Lawrence and Clare paid that price—the price of conversion and faithful love. We can still call it: *surrender*, trust in our Lord Jesus Christ.

Are we willing to say: *Jesus, I trust in you!*

5. Mercy: God's Greatest Attribute

If we read the encyclical *Dives in Misericordia* ("Rich in Mercy"), we see how Pope John Paul II recognizes *mercy as God's greatest attribute*. We also see how it is impossible to overemphasize God's mercy in the world. How important the message of mercy is to the people of our time! How much does the world, how much do you and I need the mercy of God!

The text that was the inspiration for Pope John Paul II in writing his encyclical is St. Paul's Letter to the Ephesians: "But God, who is rich in mercy, because of the great love he had for us, even when we were dead in our transgressions, brought us to life with Christ (by grace you have been saved), raised us up with him, and seated us with him in the heavens in Christ Jesus, that in the ages to come he might show the immeasurable riches of his grace in his kindness to us in Christ Jesus. For by grace you have been saved through faith, and this is not from you; it is the gift of God; it is not from works, so no one may boast" (Eph 2:4–9).

God's Love in the Face of Our Sinfulness

Mercy is, in effect, *God's love in the face of our sinfulness*. Love plus misery equals mercy. Throughout the Old Testament, God revealed his love. He revealed his kindness. He revealed his patience in the face of an often rebellious people. In other words, God revealed his mercy. The Psalms express so eloquently the theme of mercy. They give us words with which we are able to formulate the sentiments of our own hearts: I trust in the mercy of God forever and ever (cf. Ps 52:10). King David knew how to throw himself on the mercy of God and ask God's forgiveness. We have that beautiful expression in Psalm 51: "Have mercy on me, God, in your goodness; / in your abundant compassion blot out my offense. / Wash away all my guilt; / from my sin cleanse me."

In her great hymn, the Magnificat, our Blessed Mother Mary speaks about the mercy that has been revealed by God: the mercy with which Israel has been treated. Her beautiful words are: "The Mighty One has done great things for me, / and holy is his name. / His mercy is from age to age / to those who fear him.... / He has helped Israel his servant, / remembering his mercy, / according to his promise to our fathers, / to Abraham and to his descendants forever" (Luke 1:49–50, 54–55).

What is so important in Mary's Magnificat is that she recognizes God's promise of mercy to his people. Mercy was God's gift in the Old Testament; the fullness of mercy is God's gift to us in the New Testament. Mercy passes through the humanity of Christ and is made available to us in the heart of Jesus, which is the tabernacle of mediation between God and man.

Jesus himself emphasizes *the supreme importance of mercy*. At the time of the call of Matthew, Jesus was willing to answer the objection of why he would eat with tax collectors and sinners. His answer was: "Those who are well do not need a physician, but the sick do. Go and learn the meaning of the words 'I desire mercy, not sacrifice.' I did not come to call the righteous but sinners" (Matt 9:12–13).

A very beautiful sign of the times is the emphasis on mercy, the respect that the church gives to these words of Jesus: "I desire mercy." This desire for mercy Jesus makes abundantly clear in the gospels. It is his message; it is his commandment. Jesus wants to instill in us a new attitude.

One of the key texts in the gospels, to understand Jesus' own attitude toward mercy, is found in the eighteenth chapter of St. Matthew. In the context of God's mercy it is extremely important. Jesus answered Peter's question about how often he should forgive his brother. Jesus makes clear that there should be no limit, but he then goes on to explain this in the parable of the servant. The king decided to settle accounts with his servants. There was one who had no way of paying back what he owed his master. The man pleaded for mercy. The king forgave him. Jesus explained that the master was moved by compassion. But then the servant went out and found one of his fellow servants who owed him a much smaller amount. He seized him and began to choke him, demanding that he pay back what he owed. The fellow servant pleaded for compassion. It was denied. The master heard about it and summoned the servant. He expressed to him his anger and called him "you wicked servant." The master explained to the servant that he had received mercy and had refused to give it to someone else. The story ends with anger on the part of the master who handed the servant over to the torturers; at the same time Jesus draws a very explicit conclusion: "So will my heavenly Father do to you, unless each of you forgives his brother from his heart" (Matt 18:35).

The story shows the absolute insistence of Christ: his insistence that the church show mercy, that each one of us show mercy. At the same time, the story ratifies his willingness to forgive our debts and to fill us with compassion and love.

Need for Mercy

Earlier this century in Poland, God raised up a woman called Sister Faustina Kowalska. She was chosen to be a messenger and an apostle of divine mercy at a time when the world was beginning to experience an anguished need for mercy. Sister Faustina recalls the mission of St. Margaret Mary Alacoque in the church. It was as if Faustina had been chosen to make even more explicit the message that St. Margaret Mary had proclaimed in the seventeenth century regarding the heart of Jesus. Saint Margaret Mary gave her life to make known the love of the sacred heart. Faustina was called upon by God to emphasize in the twentieth century that *the love of Christ is a forgiving love, a merciful love.*

23

The message of revelation does not change with the centuries. But God continues to raise up in successive generations new messengers and apostles to proclaim his love.

The destiny of Sister Faustina is intertwined with that of John Paul II, the pope who wrote the encyclical on mercy. As archbishop of Krakow, he introduced her cause for beatification. There were difficulties and delays; we might even say reversals. But in the providence of God, it was the lot of Pope John Paul II to beatify her just a few years ago and subsequently to canonize her. The beatification took place on April 18, 1993, the Second Sunday of Easter—the day that the church proclaims the gospel of Christ's merciful love in instituting the sacrament of penance. Seven years later the Holy Father canonized her on Divine Mercy Sunday 2000.

The message that St. Faustina continues to give to the church is stupendous. It is a message already divinely revealed in the scriptures, but a message that needs to be emphasized over and over again in this century. The message of St. Faustina is the message of the gospels *that Jesus forgives*, that he has the power to forgive, that he wants his message of forgiveness to be accepted, and that *he wants us to forgive*. Jesus not only wants us to forgive, but he wants us, in our forgiving and in our personal need for forgiveness, *to trust in his merciful love*. His love comes to meet us in our infirmities, our weaknesses and our sins.

Through the beatification and canonization of Sister Faustina, the church has once again confirmed the relevance of the message of mercy in this day and age in the history of salvation. God is telling us again that grace is more powerful than sin. He is telling us that all sin can be forgiven, indeed that *sins are nothing compared with his mercy*. Obviously, the message of mercy requires renunciation on our part, the renunciation of sin. To acknowledge our sins and the power of Christ to forgive them is not to wallow in our sins; it is rather to repent of our sins and to trust that Jesus will forgive us, as we forgive others.

Mercy and Trust

In the *Diary of St. Faustina*, we see how much Jesus wanted her to understand his mercy. Her great prayer inspired by Jesus himself was this: *Jesus, I trust in you!*

One of the most beautiful pages of her autobiography includes a dialogue with Jesus. Jesus speaks to Faustina and at a given moment tells her, in effect, that she has given him so much; she has given him her life, her love, her good works and all her efforts to be holy. But Jesus says to Faustina, *there is something that you have not yet given me*. She asks what this is. And Jesus replies, expressing these sentiments: "You have not given me what is so peculiarly and specifically your own. You must entrust your weaknesses and sinfulness to my mercy." Jesus does not ask for our sins; he asks for us to entrust our lives the way they are to his mercy. He asks us to renounce sin, but nevertheless to be convinced that his mercy is able to obliterate all our sins, that his blood is able to wash away all our sins. In the words of St. John: "He is expiation for our sins, and not for our sins only but for those of the whole world" (1 John 2:2).

Christ's message of mercy is something that is *supremely relevant* to all of us. It is the message of the sacred scriptures, it is the message of God's magnificent revelation, it is the message of the church, it is the message of God's saints. It was the message of our Blessed Mother and it remains forever the teaching of Jesus who says: "Go and learn the meaning of the words, 'I desire mercy. . . .'"

Cannot each one of us summarize this teaching of mercy and express it in our dialogue of love with Christ saying: *Jesus, I trust in you!*

6. The Mystical Body

It is important to speak frequently about the Father, the Son and the Holy Spirit, about the Most Blessed Trinity. We know that from all eternity God is a Father. The Father's life is to generate the Son. The Son's life is to exist for his Father, to be the Son, to be the image, the expression, the Word, the splendor of the Father's glory and the object of his infinite and eternal love as his only begotten Son. This is the glorious title of the second person of the Most Blessed Trinity. Here the mystery begins but it does not end. In the providence of God, it was up to St. Paul to explain to the world how the only begotten Son was at the same time the firstborn Son.

Saint Paul has a beautiful phrase. He says: "For those he foreknew he also predestined to be conformed to the image of his Son, so that he might be the firstborn among many brothers" (Rom 8:29).

Here St. Paul introduces us to the wonderful design of God's love: the design of God's love manifested in his adopting us as his children, placing us on the level of his only begotten Son, causing us to live in his Son. God, therefore, wills that the sonship of his only begotten Son be shared; *that we all by grace become Jesus!* God wills to assemble us into the family of those who are brothers and sisters of Christ.

God's Plan

The church is God's plan for all of us *to be by grace his sons and daughters*, but even more *to be his only Son*. The church is the assembly, the community of those who are one in Christ the Son.

The church comes forth from the love of the Father in the Most Blessed Trinity. Quoting St. Cyprian, the Second Vatican Council says: "The Church shines forth as 'a people made one with the unity of the Father, the Son and the Holy Spirit'" (*Lumen Gentium*, 4).

The church has many names. She is called a sheepfold. She is called God's field, God's building, our Mother. The church is called the people of God, the bride of Christ. She is called the body of Christ, the mystical body of Christ.

What emerges in all these titles of the church, which try to express a profound reality that is greater than any one description or definition can contain, is *a deep relationship to Christ*. The church is Christ's and through Christ and in the Holy Spirit the church is related to the Father. For the Father, there is, moreover, *an identification of the church with his beloved Son Jesus*.

Saint Paul's Explanation

The particular title, *body of Christ* or *mystical body of Christ*, explains very well how the church is related

28

to Christ, how the church is Christ. Three times in the New Testament we hear recounted the event of Saul's conversion on the way to Damascus. Saul, who later became St. Paul, was making his way to Damascus in order to persecute the Christians. During that journey to Damascus he had a profound experience that would mark his entire life. He was knocked down and heard a voice saying to him: "Saul, Saul why are you persecuting me?" And Saul asked: "Who are you, sir?" And the voice came back: "I am Jesus the Nazorean whom you are persecuting." Saul knew that he was not persecuting Jesus of Nazareth; rather, he was persecuting the Christians. And yet the voice identified Christians with Christ: "I am Jesus the Nazorean whom you are persecuting" (Acts 22:7–8; cf. also Acts 9 and 26).

This experience profoundly touched Paul. It was the cause of his conversion. As a result of this experience, he was baptized and became the great apostle to the Gentiles. For years later he reflected on what happened and, under the inspiration of the Holy Spirit, he sought to explain the reality that he had heard proclaimed to him: "Saul, Saul why are you persecuting me?" And after long reflection and prayerful thought, Saul decided that it was possible to explain this reality, this relationship with Christ, by using the analogy of a human body. And so Paul wrote that the church is the body of Christ. The church is many, made up of many members, but is still one. It is one body, it is Christ. Christ is the head of the body; he claims it for his own and identifies himself with it.

But the church is *Christ extending himself in work and prayer throughout the ages.* This is, in effect, the role of the church, the body of Christ. All of us who have been baptized have the privilege of belonging to this body of Christ and being related to the head. The body of Christ is another name for *God's* family, which is so intimately united with Christ that it is a unity: Christ is the head and we are the members. For us, the church is Christ, our head; for the Father, the church is Christ, his beloved Son. The Father looks upon the church and loves the church as he loves his only begotten Son. The church—which we call the mystical body of Christ to distinguish it from his physical body—is the great creation of God's love whereby we live in Christ and collaborate with him, working for the salvation and sanctification of the church.

Collaborating with Christ

At this point I would like to speak about our collaboration in the church. This collaboration is very important and I would like to explain it in the words of Pope Pius XII in his encyclical on the church, *Mystici Corporis.* What do we mean when we say that *Christ needs us?* The Pope explained this in these words: "As Jesus hung on the Cross he not only avenged the justice of the eternal Father... but he also won for us, his brothers and sisters, an unending flow of graces. It was possible for him personally, immediately, to impart these graces; but he wished to do so only through a visible Church that would be formed by the union of people, and thus, through the Church, every individual would perform a work of collaboration with him in dispensing the graces of redemption. The Word of God willed to make use of our nature, when in excruciating agony, he would redeem mankind; in much the same way, throughout the centuries, he makes use of the Church so that the work begun might endure."

The pope went on to clarify this very important principle saying: "Because Christ the Head holds such an eminent position, one must not think that he does not need the Body's help. What Paul said of the human organism is to be applied likewise to the Mystical Body: 'The Head cannot say to the feet: "I have no need of you!"' It is manifestly clear that the faithful need the help of the Divine Redeemer for He has said: 'without me you can do nothing.' And in the teaching of the Apostle, every advance of this Body toward its perfection derives from Christ, the Head. Yet, this too must be held, marvelous though it appear: Christ needs his members."

This truth—that Christ needs his members—is stupendous. It was spoken more than fifty years ago, and incidentally this encyclical was one of the rich sources of the documentation of the Second Vatican Council. How impressive is this truth: *Christ needs his members!*

Pope Pius XII then further explained: "Jesus Christ wishes to be helped by the members of his Body. This is not because he is indigent and weak, but rather because he has so willed it for the greater glory of his unspotted Spouse. Dying on the Cross, Christ left to his Church the immense treasury of the redemption. Toward this she contributed nothing. But, when those graces come to be distributed, not only does Christ share this task of sanctification with his Church, but he wants it, in a way, to be due to her action."

This leads us to understand *the value of our collaboration in the church*. The pope helps us to do this by saying: "Deep mystery this, and subject of inexhaustible meditation: that the salvation of many people depends on the prayers and the voluntary penance which the members of the Mystical Body of Jesus Christ offer for this intention, and on the assistance of pastors of souls, and of the faithful, especially of fathers and mothers of families which they must offer to our Divine Savior as his associates" (*Mystici Corporis*, 16; 54–55). In all of this the main point is that we are all *valued associates in the work of Christ*, assisting him in the application of his work of redemption.

If the Father has loved us so much as to constitute his Son as the firstborn of many brothers and sisters, if the Son has loved us so much as to die for us that we might be collaborators in his body, associates in his own mission of salvation, if the Holy Spirit has loved us so much as to bring about our sanctification in the church, then *surrender to God* makes sense and our response of love and sacrifice to his call also makes profound sense.

What a privilege it is to be used by Christ as his collaborators in the salvation and sanctification of the world! How mind-boggling to realize that "this too must be held, marvelous though it appear: Christ needs his members." This means that Christ needs us and he needs us to trust in him. *Jesus, I trust in you!*

7. Faith:
Total Acceptance of Jesus

In the last verses of the Gospel of St. Mark we find the risen Jesus appearing to the eleven apostles. Saint Mark says that the apparition took place at table. The message that Jesus gave to the Eleven at that time is extremely important. He said to them: "Go into the whole world and proclaim the gospel to every creature. Whoever believes and is baptized will be saved; whoever does not believe will be condemned" (Mark 16:15–16). These words give us an understanding of *the importance Jesus attaches to faith.*

In other contexts Jesus gives us further insights into the supreme importance of faith. In the Gospel of St. John, for example, he says: "Amen, amen, I say to you, whoever believes has eternal life" (John 6:47). And earlier in the same gospel he identifies himself as the object of our faith, saying: "Whoever believes in the Son has eternal life, but whoever disobeys the Son will not see life, but the wrath of God remains upon him" (John 3:36).

The whole Christian tradition has understood these words of Jesus. The author of the Letter to the Hebrews says very clearly: "Without faith it is impossible to please [God]" (Heb 11:6).

In the sixteenth century, the church gave us a wonderful gift in the Council of Trent. And the Council of Trent gave us a wonderful presentation of faith. We recall one of the famous texts of the Council of Trent that tells us: "Faith is the beginning of human salvation, the foundation and root of all justification" (D.S., *Enchiridion Symbolorum* 1532). We can see why it is so important for us to have a deep understanding of faith and to reflect upon our own faith.

An Assent to the Testimony of the Father and the Son

It is important for us to clarify our own notion of faith. To do this we ask ourselves: *What is faith?* There are many different aspects to faith, but we know that it is truly an assent on our part—*an assent to the testimony of God the Father*, who proclaims that Jesus is his Son. We remember those wonderful words at the baptism of Jesus that God the Father spoke. It was one of those three times in the history of the world that the voice of the heavenly Father has been heard: "This is my beloved Son, with whom I am well pleased" (Matt 3:17). The acceptance that we give to Jesus, the assent that we express in regard to his divinity and his humanity is truly an echo of these words of the heavenly Father. It is faith.

At the same time the assent that we give to Jesus is also an echo of the testimony that Jesus gives about himself. Our assent to him echoes the eternal truth that he proclaims in regard to his own person. And so Jesus says to us as he said to the Jews: "Amen, amen, I say to you, before Abraham came to be, I AM" (John

8:58). Our faith is then the acceptance of these words. Our faith is *an unconditioned assent to this testimony of Jesus himself*.

There are so many other occasions in the gospels when Jesus proclaims his identity. Jesus, speaking to Martha later on in the Gospel of St. John, says to her: "I am the resurrection and the life; whoever believes in me, even if he dies, will live, and everyone who lives and believes in me will never die. Do you believe this?" (John 11:25–26). And by faith we reply to Jesus saying: we do believe. By faith we echo his words and repeat his divine testimony; we proclaim that he is indeed the resurrection and the life.

Assent to the Testimony of the Church

Once again faith is not only the assent to the testimony to the Father, it is not only the assent to the testimony of the Son, it is also the assent to the testimony of the church that is made possible by the indwelling of the Holy Spirit.

By faith we are able to express the belief of the entire church that was expressed so beautifully by Peter in the region of Caesarea Philippi. Jesus had asked his disciples: "Who do people say that the Son of Man is?" (Matt 16:13). And it was Peter who answered with such clarity and precision: "You are the Messiah, the Son of the living God" (v. 16).

By faith we participate in this testimony of Peter and at the same time we accept the judgment that Jesus expressed in regard to this profession of faith.

He said to Peter: "Blessed are you, Simon son of Jonah. For flesh and blood has not revealed this to you, but my heavenly Father" (v. 17).

Assent to the divinity of Christ and acceptance of Jesus in the fullness of his personhood are conditions for union with Christ. Faith is therefore *the acceptance of Jesus in the full reality of his being*, in his total identity as Son of God, Son of Mary and Savior of the world.

This acceptance of Jesus is what we mean by faith. To believe in Jesus is to accept him totally, to accept his word, to accept his church, to accept his incarnation and the principle that he lives in humanity, to accept his sacraments, to accept his love and pardon, to accept him not only in theory, but in practice, to choose him in the practical decisions of life, to accept him in the midst of temptations, trials and difficulties, to embrace him with his cross. And finally, *the acceptance of Jesus means the rejection of sin*.

Saint John tells us: "To those who did accept him he gave power to become children of God, to those who believe in his name..." (John 1:12). Saint Paul powerfully reasserts this doctrine contained in St. John's Gospel when he says in his Letter to the Galatians: "For through faith you are all children of God in Christ Jesus" (Gal 3:26).

And if we are children of God through this faith in Christ Jesus, and if we believe that the gift of faith is offered to all people, to the extent that all people potentially can be incorporated into Christ Jesus and by faith embrace him, then we see the great value of *accepting Christ in everyone*.

Condition for Holiness

Throughout the gospels we see how Jesus requires faith as an indispensable condition for his being willing to work miracles. Jesus requires faith in us in order for us to participate effectively in his work. Faith is a requirement for *the supernatural fruitfulness of our activities*. If God is going to produce miracles of grace through our collaboration in the hearts of other people, he must find in our own hearts the fullness of faith.

In the eleventh chapter of St. John we have the miracle of the raising of Lazarus from the dead. We have the dialogue between Jesus and Martha to which I have already alluded. What is so important is that after Jesus has declared that he is the resurrection and the life, he says to Martha: "Do you believe this?" And Martha replies: "Yes, Lord. I have come to believe that you are the Messiah, the Son of God, the one who is coming into the world" (John 11: 26–27). It is only after Martha has professed her belief in him, and only after Jesus himself has invoked his Father that he performs the miracle and calls Lazarus from the dead.

Faith is for us a sharing in the testimony of the Father about his Son and the complete acceptance of this testimony: "Whoever believes in the Son of God has this testimony within himself" (1 John 5:10). The object of our faith is Jesus Christ: Son of God, Son of Mary, Word Incarnate, Savior of the world, head of the church. And because we accept Jesus in his incarnation and in his church, faith becomes for us the great inspiration of our mission. Recognizing Christ in others, we endeavor to serve him in others, acknowledging him in the body that he took on in his incarnation, ministering to him in his poor, in those in need, in sinners. And because there is a connection between faith and eternal life, there is a connection between those whom we serve by faith and the eternal life that God gives us, rewarding us for our faithful service.

Faith becomes for us the condition for our holiness, *the cause of eternal life*. At the Last Supper Jesus prayed in a very special way for his disciples and he prayed that the world might believe that he was sent by the Father. Those beautiful words are: "I pray not only for them, but also for those who will believe in me through their word, so that they may all be one, as you, Father, are in me and I in you, that they also may be in us, that the world may believe that you sent me" (John 17:20–21).

Our lives are not compartmentalized. There is *an intimate relationship between faith and holiness in our lives*. It is from the profound conviction that Christ is God and that he has been given to us as "wisdom from God, as well as righteousness, sanctification, and redemption" (1 Cor 1:30) that we are able to pursue lives of holiness in the service of Christ and his people.

The act of faith is the very foundation of our spiritual life. If this act is frequently renewed, then Christ, as St. Paul said, "dwells in [our] hearts through faith"

(Eph 3:17). In our daily lives, we are called upon not only to accept the identity of Christ, but also to give great emphasis to the value of Christ's merits. It is he who is the cause of our holiness: it is he who has merited holiness for us, he who is the example of our holiness and he who actually brings it about in our hearts. Our acceptance of Christ is the acceptance of the Christ who calls us to holiness and makes us holy.

"Although You Have Not Seen Him, You Love Him."

One final word about faith. Faith, as we know from the experience of our Christian lives, is not vision. Faith is the condition of our earthly lives, and it is meant to yield to the vision of heaven, in which our acceptance of Christ will be complete and our possession of him total. In the meantime, St. Peter tells us that we are to rejoice. His words are very important for us as a final reflection on faith: "In this you rejoice, although now for a little while you may have to suffer through various trials, so that the genuineness of your faith, more precious than gold that is perishable even though tested by fire, may prove to be for praise, glory and honor at the revelation of Jesus Christ. Although you have not seen him you love him; even though you do not see him now, yet you believe in him, you rejoice with an indescribable and glorious joy, as you attain the goal of [your] faith, the salvation of your souls" (1 Pet 1:6–9).

This then is our faith: the acceptance of Jesus and everything about him. We accept him in the Most Blessed Trinity and in the conditions of the present moment, with his promises for the future. We accept him with trust—*Jesus, I trust in you!*—yearning for salvation for ourselves and others.

8. Jesus, I Trust in You!

The Book of Wisdom gives us a vivid summary of the night that God liberated his people. It was a night of great expectation for them. They awaited freedom and salvation.

The Book of Wisdom also draws our attention to *the promises made by God*. What gave the people courage was these promises as they were expressed in God's word and accepted in faith. Only by reason of faith were they able to live in the hope of salvation and with trust.

In the Letter to the Hebrews, *faith manifests itself as obedience, abandonment and trust* that what was promised to Abraham would come about. We have the magnificent description of faith given us: "Faith is the realization of what is hoped for and evidence of things not seen" (Heb 11:1). Abraham exemplified this confident assurance of the things hoped for. He had been called by God and sent forth to a place that he was to receive as a heritage. He did not know where he was going, and yet he was willing to go, willing to trust.

By faith Abraham sojourned in the promised land. He believed that God would fulfill his promises to him, even though he did not know how those promises were to be fulfilled. The great promise to Abraham was that he was to have a progeny as numerous as the stars in the sky. There was no way for Abraham to see how this would take place, and yet the promise was fulfilled.

The author says: "So it was that there came forth from one man...descendants as numerous as the stars in the sky and as countless as the sands on the seashore" (v. 12). Speaking then of Abraham, Isaac and Jacob, the author says: "All these died in faith. They did not receive what had been promised but saw it and greeted it from afar" (v. 13).

As our father in faith, Abraham bequeaths to us his trust that God's plan will be realized in our lives. We know that Jesus also asks us to have trust. He says in the gospel: "Do not live in fear, little flock." He lets us know that God has promised us a kingdom and yet we must await this kingdom. Meanwhile, we must divest ourselves of everything that is incompatible with the kingdom. Jesus says: "Sell your belongings and give alms" (Luke 12:33).

A very important aspect in all Christian living is *expectation*—waiting and watching and working for the coming of the kingdom. In the Mass we have the words that we hear so often: "...as we wait in joyful hope." *Our joyful hope comes from our faith*, from the confident assurance that God gives us that his plan will be realized and that our collaboration in this plan is important.

Today we renew our faith in Jesus Christ, the Incarnate Word: the one who has already come into the world, but whose Second Coming we as Christians await in joyful hope.

We look to God's promises of liberation and salvation, forgiveness and mercy, knowing that what God is asking of us in a very special way is *trust* in him.

We remember how the saints promoted trust in God. Saint Faustina Kowalska made it so much a part of her life to please Jesus by repeating the words: "*Jesus, I trust in you!*" We have the wonderful opportunity to live intensely in "the confident assurance" of our faith in Jesus Christ, the Son of God and the Son of Mary.

We are all on a journey and are called to trust in Jesus and in his Father. We are called to trust in the Holy Spirit to guide us and to assimilate us ever more to Jesus Christ, who is "the Way, the Truth and the Life" (cf. John 14:6).

God is greatly pleased when *our faith manifests itself in trust*. He has said: "More will be asked of a person to whom more has been entrusted." We have received much, let us trust greatly.

Jesus, I trust in you!

9. Baptism

Death to Sin and Life to God

During one of his visits to Poland there is a moving photograph of Pope John Paul II in prayer before the old baptismal font where he was baptized, in the parish of his birth.

Let us think of him present with us today sharing our reflections, inciting us to love for our Christian baptism. And let us think, too, of those who were present at our own baptism, those who brought us to the font of grace and life—our parents in particular— many of whom have already inherited the fruit of faith and baptism, which is eternal life.

As we have seen, faith is so important for us in our Christian life. And yet we know it is not enough. As we saw in the Gospel of St. Mark, Jesus said to his disciples: "Go into the whole world and proclaim the gospel to every creature. Whoever believes and is baptized will be saved; whoever does not believe will be condemned" (Mark 16:15–16).

Baptism is part of God's plan. It was clearly set forth by Jesus also in his conversation with Nicodemus: "Amen, amen, I say to you, no one can see the kingdom of God without being born from above." And then Jesus went on to explain his thought: "Amen, amen, I say to you, no one can enter the kingdom of

God without being born of water and Spirit" (John 3:3, 5).

Under the inspiration of the Holy Spirit the church has embraced these words of Jesus and during the centuries has proclaimed the importance of Christian baptism. Saint Paul understood profoundly this mystery that he describes in different ways. Above all, he explains to the Christians of his time the relationship that baptism sets up with Christ himself. And so linking faith and baptism, he says: "For through faith you are all children of God in Christ Jesus. For all of you who were baptized into Christ have clothed yourselves with Christ" (Gal 3:26–27).

Union with Christ and His Church

Baptism is *the sacrament of our divine adoption into Christ*. It is the first sacrament of *our Christian initiation into his Body, the church*. By baptism we become members of the church because we are united with the head of the church, our Lord Jesus Christ. Baptism realizes the eternal design of the Father to make us sons and daughters in his only begotten Son, to constitute us as brothers and sisters of Christ, to bring us into the family of Christ. In the sacrament of baptism the words of Saint John in his First Letter are fully realized: "See what love the Father has bestowed on us that we may be called the children of God. Yet so we are" (1 John 3:1).

The Father's plan is indeed glorious. The sacrament of baptism has a double aspect for us: it is the sacrament of *death to sin* and *life to God*. These two elements are so prominent in the teaching of St. Paul; these two elements are the elements of all holiness; these two elements are effected by the sacramental action of Christ in baptism. The effect of our baptism is that we become *a new creature in Christ*. Saint Paul says: "So whoever is in Christ is a new creation: the old things have passed away; behold, new things have come" (2 Cor 5:17).

Baptism is the way that God's eternal plan of predestination is carried out in our lives. It is the way that we who have been chosen in Christ are in effect *conformed to the image of his Son*. Baptism is the means whereby the family of God is constituted—the family in which Christ becomes the firstborn.

It is important for us to emphasize that what baptism symbolizes it also brings about. In baptism the immersion in water expresses *the death and burial of Jesus*. We go into the water to express our sharing in his death and burial; we come forth as a new creature, participating in *his resurrection and new life*. But baptism not only symbolizes death and resurrection, it also brings them about. It is the sacrament of our death to sin. It is the sacrament of our life to God.

In the liturgy we say so often: "By dying you destroyed our death and by rising your restored our life." Through baptism the death of Christ is operative in us and destroys sin in us. Through baptism the resurrection of Christ is operative in us and produces new life in us.

Saint Paul's Letter to the Romans explains this in a very beautiful way. He challenges the Christians of

Rome saying: "How can we who died to sin yet live in it? Or are you aware that we who were baptized into Christ Jesus were baptized into his death? We were indeed buried with him through baptism into death, so that, just as Christ was raised from the dead by the glory of the Father, we too might live in newness of life.... If, then, we have died with Christ, we believe that we shall also live with him. We know that Christ, raised from the dead, dies no more; death no longer has power over him" (Rom 6:2–4, 8–9).

The practical challenge of our baptism is explained so clearly by St. Paul, who, speaking of Christ, says: "As to his death he died to sin once and for all; as to life, he lives for God" (Rom 6:10). And then he shows that this is the whole meaning and program of our own baptism: "Consequently, you too must think of yourselves as [being] dead to sin and living for God in Christ Jesus" (v. 11).

A Call to Conversion, Holiness and Life

In effect baptism is *a call to conversion, holiness and life*. This, in effect, is what Christian living is. It is a call to death to sin; it is a call to life in Christ and this call can only be accepted through conversion— conversion based on faith. *Holiness is nothing else than the total enactment of our baptismal calling.*

Our work in Christian living is, with God's great grace, to guard the gift of divine life that has been implanted in our souls, to collaborate generously and zealously with Christ, and to serve others in the name of Christ.

In his chapter on baptism, blessed Columba Marmion, a great Benedictine spiritual writer, makes this comment: *"Christian life is nothing else but the progressive and continuous development, the practical application, throughout our whole life, of this double supernatural result of 'death' and of 'life' produced by Baptism.* There is all the program of Christianity. In the same way too our final beatitude is nothing else but the total and definitive freedom from sin, death and suffering, and the glorious unfolding of the divine life sown in us when we received this sacrament" (*Christ, the Life of the Soul*, p. 162).

The personal ratification of the promises of our baptism is of great importance. This ratification presupposes a renewed reflection on the great reality of divine adoption and Christian initiation. It presupposes a greater understanding of the challenge of Christian life, the challenge of surrender, the challenge of service. In our dialogue of love with Jesus, we are invited to speak to him about the enormous gift that we have been given: the gift of your baptism. Let us speak to his Father about his great plan of predestination, the eternal decree by which he chose us in Christ to receive baptism. Let us renew our sentiments of gratitude also to the Holy Spirit by whose action the forgiveness of sin was communicated to us through the waters of baptism, and by whose action we were introduced to new and eternal life in Christ.

Baptismal Consecration and Mission

There are then three sentiments that are particularly fitting for us now. *Gratitude* to the Most Blessed Trinity: Father, Son and Holy Spirit. But also *joy* and *confidence*. Death to sin and life to God evoke in us the most profound joy and the greatest confidence that we could possibly have. Think of it: we have the right to present ourselves confidently to Jesus, saying: *Jesus, I trust in you!* We can also present ourselves to our heavenly Father in the name of Jesus, and we can do so *as Christ Jesus*. Remember, we are not only sons and daughters; we are, by the grace of divine adoption of our baptismal consecration, configured to *the* Son. We are configured to the *only* Son. Christ looking on us says: "Me," as he said to Saul about his followers: "Why are you persecuting *me*?" (Acts 9:4, emphasis added). And the Father looking on each of us says: "This is my beloved Son" (Matt 3:17).

Because of our identification with Christ—by grace not by nature—we must realize the immense value of our prayer, our worship, our suffering, our daily acts, all the activities of our lives. We have "put on" Christ. We live for God as his beloved children, in the Son, who has given his life so that we might live with him for the glory of his Father in union with the Holy Spirit.

And finally we must not forget the immense challenge that is ours—the challenge of effectively dying to sin, or rejecting sin, as is required by our baptism; the challenge of not taking the body of Christ, our own body, and sinning with it. There are many applications of the doctrine of baptism to our lives. One of them is the challenge of not being guilty of omission. The Christ who lives in us, the Son to whom we have been incorporated and to whom we have been configured, wishes to work and to love in us.

The last great challenge of our baptism is *the challenge of service* in the world. Remember the Jesus to whom we belong said this: "The Son of Man did not come to be served but to serve and to give his life as a ransom for many" (Matt 20:28).

There are two more thoughts that I would like to share with you. The first is that this new ecclesial life that we have received in baptism is the basis of everything that we are and do; it is the basis for our own life and mission.

Finally, baptism opens up to us the great mystery of eternal life, which is our inheritance. Saint John tells us: "Beloved, we are God's children now; what we shall be has not yet been revealed. We do know that when it is revealed we shall be like him, for we shall see him as he is" (1 John 3:2).

Dear friends: we see what love the Father has bestowed on us, and it has all come to us through the heart of Jesus.

10. Sin: Refusal of Love

We can never reflect sufficiently on the fact that Christian life means *death to sin* and *life to God*. This is in effect the meaning of our baptism; this is in effect the definition of our holiness.

And now we turn to sin. What is this reality in our lives? What is sin? We know that it is a thought, word, act or omission that goes contrary to the divine plan for humanity—the plan the Father has formulated in his Eternal Word. In other words, sin is a violation of God's law. It is likewise a personal, a free *no* spoken to God: an offense against the persons of the Most Blessed Trinity. As a response to the unlimited love of God poured out in our hearts by the Holy Spirit, sin defies understanding: it is *the mystery of iniquity*.

Sin and Human Freedom

Before going any further, permit me to recount one version of a story attributed to Leonardo da Vinci, the great Italian genius, and creator of, among other works, *The Last Supper*. I had the privilege many years ago of visiting *The Last Supper* in Milan. Since that time, I know that the painting deteriorated greatly!

The story is told, however, that the artist created that famous masterpiece by painting Christ and the apostles from different human models that were presented to him. And as the story goes, Leonardo da Vinci finally had the entire painting completed; that is the entire painting except for Christ and Judas. He was waiting to have the appropriate models that would express the characteristics that he wanted to find in both Christ and Judas. He waited, it is said, for a number of years, so he could finally find someone worthy of Christ, someone whom he could paint and who, for him, would express the goodness and the holiness that he wanted his "Christ" to possess in the painting. Finally he found this person, and the painting was complete, except for Judas!

And so the search went on and time went by. Finally, Da Vinci came upon the person whom he thought would be the proper subject to model Judas. It was obvious that he had found a person who did not exemplify virtue, who did not at least give the impression of leading a virtuous life. And so Leonardo was able to complete his work. The last of the apostles was sketched for the great masterpiece. And before his subject took leave of him, the person told Leonardo that, yes, they had met before; it was not the first time. As a matter of fact, his "Judas" told him that he had modeled for him some years before; indeed he had been his "Christ."

The Italians have an expression: *Se non è vero, è ben trovato!* In other words, if it is not factual, it still has a great lesson in it. And the lesson in the story is that a good person can change. A person that exemplifies and practices virtue has the freedom to say *no* to God. He or she has the freedom to change. A sinner can be converted and become a saint. A person of virtue can become a sinner. It works *both ways*. To gain some idea of sin, especially deadly sin, mortal sin, we must consider it in its different aspects. Sin displeases God. Sin is the enemy of Christ. Sin destroys divine life.

"For Our Sake He Made Him to Be Sin...."

Sin displeases God, because it is an out-and-out refusal of love, the refusal to live the truth of our relationship with God. It is the refusal of cooperating with the Father's love in living the life of Christ. Sin is the enemy of Christ because it is the instrument of his passion. We recall the extraordinary text of St. Paul in his Second Letter to the Corinthians, already alluded to. Saint Paul has those electrifying words in speaking about God the Father's action in regard to Christ: "For our sake he made him to be sin who did not know sin, so that we might become the righteousness of God in him" (2 Cor 5:21).

In the expression of St. Paul, sin *transfigures Jesus into sin* to the point that the Father, instead of glorifying his Son, as he wants to do, lays upon him the guilt of us all. *The Father made Christ who did not know sin to be sin.* This is indeed a dramatic phrase, but it is uttered under the inspiration of the Holy Spirit. This gives us some idea of the extent to which

Christ carried the burden of the world as he expiated for our sins. If we could only realize how much Christ loves his Father! He tells us that he always does what pleases his Father! And now, St. Paul tells us that the Father makes him the sin of the world. Christ is transformed into sin, becomes sin and, in becoming sin, assumes in his person the repugnance of sin. As sin he is repugnant to the Father whom he loves and to the Father who loves him. All we can say is that sin is indeed the mystery of iniquity!

Sin also destroys divine life, we said, and thus excludes us from the kingdom of God. Mortal sin severs the divine union. It is the complete rejection of Christ's invitation: "remain in my love" (John 15:9). It is a perverse use of freedom. As such it destroys divine life in our hearts, but it goes further. Sin destroys families. It can wound and destroy religious communities. Even internal sins wound the relationship of the church with Christ. Jesus has revealed that there is *eternal punishment for sin*. He tells us in Matthew's Gospel that those who reject him in others "will go off to eternal punishment, but the righteous to eternal life" (Matt 25:46). This eternal punishment the church calls *hell*. And the church guarantees us that it is a reality. Indeed, the essence of hell consists in *an eternal inextinguishable thirst for God*.

Reality of Sin

This then is the context in which we understand the evil of sin, the supreme evil of mortal sin. And if even once we have committed a mortal sin, we have merited hell because of the holiness of God. Yet we know that God's mercy is greater than sin.

As we speak about sin, we must evoke also *original sin*: the sin of Adam that is transmitted to us in its effects. We realize that original sin has placed us in a position of weakness, or frailty and concupiscence. It is as a result of original sin that we carry the treasure of divine life in fragile vessels.

The reality of original sin also helps us to understand *venial sin*, the sin that is a very real part of our life, the sin that is still truly sin. In understanding venial sin and its context, we know that human frailty, weakness of the will, the relaxing of the intensity of our love for God is one thing. Quite another thing is the cool deliberation of saying *no* to God, the lack of supernatural docility, the succession of willful negligences in small things. From the condition of a cool deliberation in expressing *no* to God in lesser matters, we can so often glide imperceptibly to the brink of grave sin. We reflect on the reality of sin and on our own commitment to die to sin in order to live in God in Christ Jesus. The opposite of sin is joyful surrender to God.

Does the church insist on *the reality of sin*? Absolutely. Is mercy still available whenever we have sinned? Of course. Is it popular to speak about sin? No, to speak about sin is not "in."

Some people in the world today are vehement in holding that the very concept of sin as a limitation to their human freedom is an offense to their human dignity. They want to be able to do anything that corresponds to their concept of freedom and not call it sin. They insist that God's unconditional love is incompatible with restrictions on their human freedom.

Does God love us unconditionally? Of course. But Jesus has also said: "You are my friends if you do what I command you" (John 15:14). Sin, the mystery of iniquity, revealed both as mortal sin and venial sin, demands our reaction and our rejection. This in turn requires *vigilance* and *prayer*, the prayer that helps us in temptation, the prayer of reparation to God, of expiation in union with Christ who was made sin by his Father. We also have the testimony of the saints to the effectiveness of prayer to our Blessed Mother to avoid sin: O Mary, conceived without sin, pray for us who have recourse to you!

Forgiveness and Pardon

Sin forces us once again to reflect on *the mercy of God*, to reflect on the mystery of forgiveness and pardon, to proclaim with St. Paul the superabundance of grace.

As Jesus places us on guard against sin, as Jesus tells us to be vigilant and to pray always, he reiterates the great mystery of God's loving kindness in the face of sin. In doing this, he permits and encourages us, sinners though we be, to have *unlimited confidence* in our heavenly Father. He encourages us to trust in him who is the lamb of God and who takes away the sins of the world to say to him: *Jesus, I trust in you!* No reflection on God's mercy can, however, justify us in remaining in our sin. The wonderful promises of God are all oriented to the fact that we are to reject sin in order to live in holiness of life. We are to turn from sin; we are to be converted and live. We are to die to sin and live to God.

In the short pontificate of Pope John Paul I, there are two extraordinary references to what I call "*the advantages of being a sinner.*" These are texts that are very beautiful and that merit study and reflection. They are extraordinary expressions of confidence in divine mercy. But what Pope John Paul I says in effect is that those who have sinned do have an advantage. Is it a motive for sinning? No. Is it a reason to wallow in our sins? Absolutely not. But in the providence of God the remembrance of the sins that we have committed can have a twofold salutary effect.

Number one: it can make us understand that we have offended God, that we have sinned and that we merit punishment. It can draw our attention to our proper relationship with God and make us sensitive to the fact that we cannot boast of ourselves. In other words, the remembrance and acknowledgement of sin can produce *an attitude of true humility* in our hearts.

And number two: we who have committed sin and been pardoned, we who have received the mercy of God are *bound to show mercy to others*. And this demonstration of mercy begins with a sensitivity to other people who have sinned, an understanding of human weakness that has nothing to do with condoning sin. It is rather, once again, the expression of the servant who has been forgiven and the servant who, having been forgiven, knows that he must forgive his fellow servants. And so humility and compassion are indeed "advantages of being a sinner."

Certainly the world today needs the virtue of humility and the virtue of compassion. And with these virtues we are more suitably prepared to approach God himself and to ask for further pardon and mercy and forgiveness.

The church does not dwell on sin. The church dwells on Christ and she concentrates on *the cross of Christ* by which all the sins of the world have been destroyed. And she concentrates on the teaching of the apostles, including those magnificent words of St. Paul that: "power is made perfect in weakness" (2 Cor 12:9). And she proclaims also with St. Paul that where sin abounded, grace did more abound, grace has overflown.

Mercy Is Stronger than Sin

In our own lives the reality of sin, the mystery of iniquity must be recognized. But we owe it to Christ to proclaim that he in his mercy is stronger than all the sins of the world, and his grace is capable not only of obliterating our sins but of keeping us from sin in the future. The renunciation of sin must be something firm in our lives because we know the price that Jesus has paid in his passion and death to take away the sins of the world.

I wish to draw attention to the fact that, in Christian living, it is not human frailty or human weakness that is an obstacle to God's grace. God knows the way we are made. What is an obstacle to God's grace is any deliberate act on our part that closes our heart to him, any willful rejection of his love. Saint Paul quotes his dialogue with Christ in which the Lord said: "My grace is sufficient for you, for power is made perfect in weakness." And St. Paul himself goes on to say: "I will rather boast most gladly of my weaknesses in order that the power of Christ may dwell with me. Therefore, I am content with weaknesses, insults, hardships, persecutions, and constraints, for the sake of Christ; for when I am weak, then I am strong" (2 Cor 12:9–10).

Our final attitude toward sin is so beautifully expressed in St. John's First Letter, where he says: "My children, I am writing this to you so that you may not commit sin. But if anyone does sin, we have an Advocate with the Father, Jesus Christ the righteous one. He is expiation for our sins, and not for our sins only but for those of the whole world. The way we may be sure that we know him is to keep his commandments" (1 John 2:1–3).

11. Mercy and the Sacrament of Penance

Every Good Friday since his election, Pope John Paul II goes in the morning to St. Peter's Basilica to hear confessions. He wants to give a witness to the world of *the importance of the sacrament of penance*, the sacrament of mercy in the life of the church.

Some people look upon the sacrament of penance as a burden, or at least a duty. It is rather *a great gift of God's mercy*. And what is mercy? It is the ocean of God's love in the face of human frailty, human misery, human sin.

Christ's Easter Gift

The sacrament of penance or reconciliation is *the Easter gift of the heart of Christ*. Let us go back to the evening of the resurrection, as described in the Gospel of St. John. Saint John comments on the fact that the doors of the upper room were locked. The disciples were in there for fear of the Jews and then Jesus came and stood in their midst and said to them: "Peace be with you" (John 20:26). What follows is the marvelous account of the institution of the sacrament of penance that remains for all time the Easter gift of Christ to his church.

The context of the institution of the sacrament of penance is very important. The apostles are gathered together and Jesus comes and meets them all together for the first time after his passion and death. We have to realize that this is the first time for the group to see Jesus after all the events of Holy Week had taken place. For Peter, it is the first meeting with Jesus after that horrible denial. For the other apostles, it is the first time they are face to face with Jesus after demonstrating their weakness during the passion. All of the apostles had run away, except John; Peter, their head, had done worse. If there ever was a moment in which the apostles were ashamed, it was that Easter evening. If there ever was a moment when Jesus had a right to upbraid them, it was the moment of that Easter encounter.

Jesus could have recalled to them their weakness as a salutary remembrance of what had taken place. He could have commented on their cowardice. He could have pointed out just how serious their abandonment of him was. And yet Jesus took another approach.

Jesus comes into the room in a moment in which they are still living in fear and at a time when his presence provokes the fullest measure of shame in them, and he says: "Peace be with you." We have to remember that the greeting of peace is for all time to be the greeting of the Easter Lord. The first message of the angels to the shepherds at the birth of Jesus was the message of peace. It was the message that summed up what would be the mission of Christ. And now the risen Christ with his mission accomplished greets his shamefaced apostles with this message. And this is the message that the church, through the apostles, will pass down throughout the ages.

Jesus saw this moment as the most propitious moment to give to his apostles *the power to forgive sins*. It was a moment in which they were supremely conscious of their weakness. It was a moment in which they were overwhelmed by a sense of their own sin. It was a moment in which they could not possibly pretend that they could forgive sins in their own name. This was the moment that Jesus chose to communicate to weak, sinful men a power they were to exercise in his church and in his name. The Easter gift of the risen Lord was to be *a legacy of mercy and forgiveness and pardon for all generations.*

Jesus repeats to the apostles the words: "Peace be with you." And then he proceeds to give them their charge. He tells them that as the Father has sent him, so he sends them. "And when he had said this, he breathed on them and said to them: 'Receive the holy Spirit. Whose sins you forgive are forgiven them, and whose sins you retain are retained'" (John 20:22–23).

Forgiveness Passes through the Humanity of Christ

Jesus had made it very clear that he was giving his apostles the power to forgive sins because of a need experienced in the church. His apostles themselves needed forgiveness. Their successors and all the members of the church would need forgiveness. At the same time Jesus made so perfectly clear that *this forgiveness came from him* and *it was to be exercised by his apostles through the power of the Holy Spirit.* The Holy Spirit, who is God's love in the Most Blessed Trinity, is *the ultimate explanation* for the forgiveness of sins. God's love is the reason that sins can be forgiven, and the very forgiveness of sins is an action on God's part that cannot be distinguished from his love, his Holy Spirit.

On that first Easter evening Jesus was proclaiming, in effect, that just as he had saved all people, acting through his sacred humanity, which was handed over to death for the redemption of the world, so he would continue through the humanity of his priests to ensure that the pardon that had been brought about in his blood would continue to be available in his church. By so doing *he ratified forever the principle of the incarnation* whereby all humanity was lifted up to a new level because the Son of God, the Eternal Word of God, assumed humanity in the womb of the Virgin Mother.

The institution of the sacrament of penance remains an expression of *the Easter triumph of Christ.* It is forever associated with his Easter victory and forever recounted as part of the Easter event. In the liturgy of the church, this reading from the Gospel of St. John that presents the institution of the sacrament of penance is proclaimed on the Second Sunday of

Easter, on the eighth day after the resurrection. In the providence of God, this Sunday after Easter speaks to us repeatedly about *God's mercy*. Especially in recent years, an enormous amount of attention has been drawn to the mystery of God's mercy on this Sunday. Saint Faustina Kowalska conveyed to the church the urgency with which, as she understood it, Jesus wished his mercy to be celebrated on that day. In 1993, Pope John Paul II chose the Second Sunday of Easter as the day to beatify Sister Faustina and to draw attention *to the celebration of Divine Mercy Sunday* in the church. On the Second Sunday of Easter, April 30, 2000, Pope John Paul II canonized Blessed Faustina.

We have already seen how sin is indeed the mystery of iniquity. At the same time we see how the sacrament of penance is truly *the mystery of mercy revealed through the sacred humanity of Christ* and poured out into the world.

At the Time of Christ's Easter Victory, We Celebrate His Merciful Love

This mystery of mercy passes through the loving and living humanity of Jesus, whose heart forever sustains his human life and symbolizes his human love. But his human life is united to the divine life in which life and love are one. And so *his heart is the expression of the life of the living God* and *the sign of the eternal love that constitutes God's life*. Passing through the humanity of Christ, this love reveals itself as mercy and becomes sacramental mercy from generation to generation. The Father has chosen the moment of sin to reveal merciful love. The Easter victory of God's power over sin becomes the moment to celebrate his merciful love.

The revelation of God's mercy is indeed the *revelation of power*—immense power: the power of God to destroy evil in human hearts. This is why the church says that God, by showing mercy and pardon, gives the greatest manifestation of his power. The Father wills that the great victory of his Son Jesus over sin and death should pass through the sacrament of penance and thus be applied to human hearts. The victory of the blood of Jesus is what is at stake. The value of the sacrament of penance is this: the blood of Jesus is applied to our souls; the victory of this blood takes effect in human hearts; and the evil of sin is effectively overcome by the love and mercy of God: Father, Son and Holy Spirit. This is why the church repeatedly proclaims with St. Paul that grace has far surpassed sin. The gift of God is far superior to the offense. The mercy and love and power of God totally surpass the evil of sin. The infinite merits of the death of Jesus take away the sins of the world; they are applied to each of us in the sacrament of penance.

For us Christians the name of Jesus signifies this: he is Savior, victory, the power of God unto salvation. Acting through the Holy Spirit, he brings about forgiveness, pardon and reconciliation in the sacrament of penance. He is the propitiation, the victim of expiation, the sacrifice of atonement for our sins and those of the whole world.

We are invited to accept this mystery of mercy and pardon in the way that God offers it through the church. It comes to us through the humanity of Jesus, through the sacrament of penance, through the humanity of the priest—but only as an instrument of Jesus the Incarnate Word. And each time we confess our sins to a priest, we express our faith in the blood of Jesus and we proclaim with our whole being that we accept the church of the Incarnate Word, we accept the humanity of Jesus and the divine plan that the principle of the incarnation embraces the person of Christ's priest. No matter how weak or sinful or unattractive the person of the priest may be, the sacrament is always an encounter with the merciful Savior—a personal encounter with the Incarnate Word and with his forgiving Father in the communion of the Holy Spirit.

Does this take faith to realize? Very much so. We are at a point of extreme importance for the life of the church, for the holiness of the church, for the salvation of the world and for the fruitfulness and authenticity of our lives. What are we being asked to do? *To accept the Father's plan*; not to change it, but to understand it, to love it, to embrace it. There is no substitute. When we enter into the divine plan, our whole life changes.

Need for Confession of Sins

Practically speaking, what does the sacrament of penance mean? It means *the admission of sin*. This involves *contrition, sorrow, a purpose of amendment,* not a guarantee, but a sincere resolve to do better with God's help. In other words, it means *conversion*.

The sacrament also involves *confession* to the Jesus who obtained pardon through his humanity and now grants his pardon through the humanity of the priest. And finally, the sacrament involves *satisfaction for sin*.

All of these elements deserve our reflection. They are, under grace, the various elements of the sacrament on the part of the penitent, to which are added *the absolution of the priest* and *the forgiveness of God*. It is God who reveals mercy, who forgives and reconciles; he it is who converts and gives grace to the penitent. The sacrament of penance exists in order to reconcile us with God. Obviously then, the sacrament is, in the case of mortal sins, a profound reconciliation. But the church knows the intention of Jesus in its totality; Jesus wills that all sins be taken away.

Venial sin obstructs the fullness of holiness, conversion and life. Venial sin weakens us in the paschal struggle and often disposes us to give in to further temptation. Also in the case of venial sin we need *a strengthening contact with the blood of Jesus*. The sacrament pardons us, confirms us in pardon and heals us, little by little, of the effects of sin. Our authentic use of the sacrament of penance also necessitates satisfaction for sin and *mortification*. The blood of Jesus with which we have contact in the sacrament of penance revives us, strengthens us, makes us generous in resisting temptation.

On a practical level, we must be patient in confessing our sins. It may be hard, it may be irksome, it may indeed be *penitential*.

Confession of Sins Is Expression of Trust

One of the greatest challenges of the postconciliar church is the renewed use of the sacrament of penance. One of our greatest challenges is to embrace Jesus in his sacrament of mercy, thus proclaiming, by example and in practice, the forgiveness and mercy of the Father that passes through the humanity of Jesus and is brought about by the action of his Spirit. We are, indeed, called to proclaim effectively that holiness is linked to the sacrament of penance. Our *frequent confession* is a gift on our part to the church, an example of our faith.

Pope Pius XII stated, and our present Holy Father has quoted him repeatedly, that it is not without the inspiration of the Holy Spirit that frequent confession was introduced into the church.

It is very important that our *call to conversion, holiness and life*, should lead us to the sacrament of penance and culminate in a renewed and more fervent celebration of the eucharistic sacrifice. I personally have repeatedly heard the Holy Father speak to so many people about the sacrament of penance. I have heard him tell the bishops to encourage the priests to go to confession and to lead the way by their own personal example.

It is important for us to avail ourselves of confession to a priest of our choice, not only during a retreat or in conjunction with it, but also as the years go on, remaining faithful to the sacrament. This means being open to the reception of God's mercy, there where Christ has ordained that it be found. To confess our sins is to proclaim effectively: *Jesus, I trust in you!*

Our Lord Jesus Christ asks us to believe in him, to accept his Easter gift, the gift that flows from his open side, the gift that is explained by his loving heart.

12. The Heart of Jesus: Inspiration and Challenge

On certain days, the church gives us the freedom to choose the particular aspect of the mystery of God that we wish to celebrate in the liturgy. It is a great privilege, therefore, to be able to celebrate often *the mystery of the sacred heart*. In doing so, we are celebrating *God's love as it passes through the humanity of Jesus and is symbolized in his heart*.

We find inspiration and challenge in the heart of Jesus. It is meant to be this way. In the prayer over the gifts in the Mass of the sacred heart we pray to God: "Look on the Heart of Christ your Son filled with love for us. Because of his love accept our Eucharist and forgive our sins."

How fortunate we are to live in the fullness of time, which includes the fullness of the revelation of God's love in the humanity of Christ, and the fullness of forgiveness.

In the heart of Jesus, *the fullness of pardon and mercy* is poured out. It was not so in the old covenant in the time of Ezekiel who witnessed the profanation of the temple and the time of punishment. We hear those terrible words spoken about those who performed abominations in the holy city: "Do not look on them with pity nor show any mercy!" (Ezek 9:5).

But we have been forgiven. We have received abundant mercy from God—*mercy without limit.* This mercy has come to us from the Father, through Jesus Christ and through the church, which has received unlimited power to forgive. This unlimited power to forgive is clearly enunciated in the Hebrew expression "to bind and to loose."

No Room for Pride

The forgiveness we have received must transform us into forgiving people. If we have been forgiven, then we have no reason to look upon ourselves as being strong in ourselves. There is no room for pride. Humility involves compunction. We remember our sins, not to doubt the forgiveness we have received, not to lack confidence in God, but to understand our true relationship to him. The acknowledgment of our sins generates in us *an attitude of humble gratitude and trust* that we express, saying: *Jesus, I trust in you!*

Christ's grace is greater than our sins and all the sins of the world. The remembrance of our own sins also means that we can understand the weaknesses of others and still not condone their sins. *We have been forgiven; we must forgive.* Forgiveness received demands in us a new attitude toward others.

In the Gospel of St. Matthew we hear the words of Jesus: "Where two or three are gathered together in my name, there am I in their midst" (Matt 18:20). Jesus truly wants to remain in our midst. He wants us to be always a community united to his heart and ever challenged by it. This means being *a people of forgiveness, mercy and patient love*, ever expressing gratitude for all the blessings flowing from the sacred heart of Jesus.

13. Christian Death

The topic of death is truly related to the resurrection of Jesus and to his victory.

We are speaking about Christian death. We are speaking about our death. This means *the death of Jesus in each one of us* as it takes place in a very real way at the moment of our own death.

Let us go back for just a moment to Luke 23:44–46, just to present this great event: the death of Jesus. It was now around midday. Darkness came over the whole land until midafternoon with an eclipse of the sun. The curtain of the sanctuary was torn in two. Jesus uttered a loud cry and said, "Father, into your hands I commend my spirit." After he said this, he bowed his head and died.

The Power to Lay Down Our Life Freely

We know the power that Jesus possessed to lay down his life freely in death. We know that he exercised this power and that he has communicated this power to us. *It is exhilarating to reflect on our power to lay down our life freely.*

But first, let us ask two questions: What did death mean to Jesus? What should it mean for us?

For Jesus, death meant the gift of himself in total trust, in sacrifice, in suffering offered to his Father, in love, in obedience, in order to effect redemption. Even though he suffered enormously, *nothing gave Jesus greater satisfaction than to die* in order that the world would know, as he said, that he loves the Father and does what the Father willed. In death, Jesus obeyed the Father perfectly; he conquered death and won life for his church. The Father accepted Jesus' total gift and ratified its redemptive value by raising Jesus from the dead.

What about us? Death is part of our lives. *Preparing for death is the greatest opportunity in our lives!* We have the possibility to rehearse our death, not in its minute details—although many saints have found this useful—but in the sense of anticipating the act of our will that will be consummated freely at the moment of our death and offered to the Father in union with the death of Jesus. We can anticipate by an act of our will the laying down of our life in union with Jesus!

The Father wills that we pass through death—redeemed death—the death that is now linked not only with sin but also with the death of Jesus and his resurrection. The Father wills that we pass through death with his Son in order to live, not in order to die, and in order to make up in our flesh what is mysteriously wanting in the passion and death of the Lord. Seen in this perspective, *death is the moment to give all, to surrender all with Jesus and in union with his sacrifice.* All of this can be anticipated by an act of our will, by an act of our love. When anticipated by an act of loving acceptance, death is an opportunity to say *yes* to the Father, just as Jesus did; to say *yes* with all our heart, as Jesus did.

Jesus first anticipated death at the moment of his incarnation. We see these sentiments in the Letter to the Hebrews where he totally and completely accepted in anticipation the death that he was going to endure. Speaking to his Father, he said: "...a body you have prepared for me; / holocausts and sin offerings you took no delight in. / Then I said... 'I have come to do your will, O God'" (Heb 10:5–7). Yes, Jesus anticipated death in the incarnation and then fully embraced it at the hour of his cross.

A Magnificent Opportunity

Death is a magnificent opportunity to be able to make up for every lack of love in our lives, for every lack of obedience, for every lack of saying *yes*, for every sin that we have ever committed. But this final moment of our lives, even in its anticipation, in the act of love by which we accept it, is so special. *Now is the time to give all!* And if we do, there is joy and peace and love in obedience, in our act of final surrender, anticipated day after day in love.

Death is for all of us the act of our final oblation, the act of the final offering of ourselves. In consenting freely to our death, we are like Jesus: *we have power!* We have the power to lay down our life, exactly as Jesus did, exactly as Jesus said: "No one takes it from me; I lay it down on my own. I have power to lay it down" (John 10:18).

For Religious, death is *the final renewal of religious profession*. It is the final offering united to the

Eucharist. It is the hour—especially when it is anticipated by many acts of the will—to assemble, and through Jesus to offer to the Father, all the acts of generosity in their lifetime, every *yes* that followed their call from the Lord and was ever expressed in their Christian life, every act of penance, every act of love that was ever manifested at any time in their youth, in their religious consecration, in their ecclesial mission!

This preparation for death, this act of the will on our part, this anticipation through love—call it what you will—also contains *a great power of expiation.* Consciously, lovingly, freely we say *yes* to the Father. We say *yes* to the definitive renunciation of our will in the most radical way possible. We accept to follow Jesus to the cross and we accept all the unknown details of a death that awaits us. We willingly ratify in advance everything in an act of love. We have power! We have the power to do this! At this moment we boast with Jesus: "I have the power to lay down my life!" He gave us this power. In this sense, no one takes it from us. We rob death by this act of our will of its ability to be only a punishment for sin. We lay down our life freely, in accordance with the Father's will. We lay it down radically, definitively, forever! Why? *So that sins may be forgiven!*

What is the conclusion to be drawn here? Truly, the acceptance of this disposition of the Father, the necessity of our dying in union with Christ, is *a special moment in our conversion.* It can be a special moment every day. It can be a special moment renewed thousands of times. It is a special step to holiness. It is a special grace of sharing in Christ's risen life. It is a special moment, too, in every retreat. This anticipation of death gives us immense joy! It gives joy to our lives. It confirms us in fervor and in love.

What Our Death Means to the Father

There are other exhilarating aspects to our death, not only what it means to us but what our death means to the Father. This is an ineffable mystery! I spoke about our anticipation of the acceptance of death. For the Father, the death of each of us is the re-enactment of the death of Jesus. We have been sacramentally configured to his Son in baptism, we have accompanied him so many times in the Eucharist, we have met him in the moment of the triumph of his blood in the sacrament of penance. The Father sees all of this, and in that hour of our death he sees and accepts our death as the death of Jesus. He sees our death as united with the death of Jesus through baptism and the Eucharist. We have been configured with the Lord Jesus and we have received the right to rise with him and to participate fully in the paschal mystery.

When the Father sees our death, our pain, our sacrifice, our resignation, our joyful and obedient acceptance, he can see nothing else but the death of his Son Jesus. In virtue of his gift to us of divine adoption, he can say: "My Jesus!" There is no other reality that exists for the Father because, before the world began, he generated us in his word, in his Eternal Word, and he predestined us to share in the paschal mystery of the crucified and risen Jesus.

Seeing our death, which is the consummation of our baptism, and seeing the death of Jesus in this death of ours, the Father is moved to apply to us personally the full salvific power of the cross and resurrection. He acknowledges and he proclaims in himself, in the communion of the Blessed Trinity, that his Son Jesus is definitively our Savior, that the blood of the lamb is gloriously victorious. This is, of course, *the most sublime aspect of our death and its preparation.* There is nothing comparable to *what our death means to the Father.*

Radical Surrender in Joyful Hope

Yet, there are other aspects, wonderful aspects that fill our souls with joy at the thought of death and at the possibility that we can prepare so personally, so often, with such freedom and such love. We know that our Blessed Mother, Mary, will be with us at the hour of death: the Queen of Angels, the Queen of Saints, the Mother of the Word Incarnate, the Mother of the Church, our Mother Mary. It will be *her last maternal act* in our regard. It will be the consummation of the love with which she loved us in her Son and kept us from the evil one and accompanied us in all our needs during life. It will be for her the hour of her supreme fidelity toward us when once again, hearing the words of Jesus on Calvary—

"Woman, behold, your son" (John 19:26)—she will express at our death the sentiments of Jesus speaking to his Father, and they will become her words: "They belonged to you, and you gave them to me, and they have kept your word" (John 17:6).

In that hour, St. Joseph, too, will exercise his intercession for our holy death as *patron of the dying*. He will respond to the call of the church to be with us, to intercede for us. As Jesus becomes definitively our Savior in the hour of our death, Joseph will recall how it was he and Mary, who, acting on instructions from the angel, gave the child the name of Jesus, which means *Savior*. Now, this is coming to pass exactly as it was foreordained. In St. Luke's Gospel, in the annunciation, we have the angel telling Mary that she would call him Jesus. In the Gospel of St. Matthew, the angel goes directly to Joseph and says, "You are to name him Jesus, because he will save his people from their sins" (Matt 1:21). Here is the moment of culmination when Jesus is Savior for each one of us, and Mary and Joseph acknowledge this in praise to the Father.

Death is the *last act of our baptismal commitment*, the final contribution that we will make to the mission of the church until our voices join the Liturgy of Heaven and are associated with the Lamb and his saints in intercession for the living.

This brings us to still another point that inspires us in joyful hope as we await the blessed hour of our death. That moment is *the true conclusion of the matrimonial graces given to our beloved parents*. Only with the final triumph of our death is their work completely achieved. All the graces that emanated from their sacramental union are now effective.

Why evoke all this? Because it is so intimately connected with the paschal mystery in us and to the Lord's call to conversion, holiness and life! The death of Jesus in us and in our death is *the cause of resurrection and eternal life*. We are called to embrace this death in order to live, to live for God in Christ Jesus our Lord. A conscious acceptance of our death in union with Jesus renewed a thousand times in our lives is the loving repetition of an act of surrender to the will of the Father. It is a radical surrender, a total surrender. It is the expression of total openness on our part to let the paschal mystery of Jesus possess us in the embrace of love. The condition is death, just as it was for Jesus.

We have power to offer with Jesus to the Father all the pains and anguish and suffering and especially the separation of body and soul that takes place in death, as our sacrifice of love and obedience and reparation for our sins. Because our sacrifice is fused with that of Jesus, it will have *redemptive value for the salvation of the world*. Our death will have sanctifying value for the church.

At his death, Jesus uttered seven words. Two of them were particularly personal to him. He called upon his Mother and his Father. He said to St. John, "Behold, your mother" (John 19:27). Finally he cried out, "Father, into your hands I commend my spirit" (Luke 23:46). We desire to die invoking Mary and enjoying her maternal relationship, just as Jesus did at the hour of his death. We also ardently desire to die presenting ourselves to the Father as brothers and sisters of Jesus, through grace identified with Jesus himself.

Our Last Proclamation, Our Last Invocation

At that final hour, if God gives us consciousness, we hope to make *the last great proclamation of our lives*. We can rehearse it; we can anticipate it so many, many times! This last great proclamation of our lives is all contained in the one word *Jesus* by which we express our trust in him—*Jesus, I trust in you!*— whom we proclaim the Savior, our Savior, Mary's Son and the eternal and beloved Son of the Father. He is the Eternal Word, the firstborn from the dead, the risen Lord who will raise us up in glory to be with the Father and Holy Spirit, with himself, in the communion of the Most Blessed Trinity, forever.

Following our last proclamation—the holy name of *Jesus*—we still aspire to make one last *invocation*. It is the word *Father*. We have been configured to the Son of God, who is the Son of Mary. We have been redeemed by his precious blood, nourished by his word and sacraments, loved by his Mother, assisted by his church. And now the moment has come to be presented by Jesus to his Father in the communion of the Holy Spirit. Our identification with Jesus has been finalized. The only word left to utter is *Father*: "Father into your hands I commend my spirit." Our identification with Jesus is complete. The Father accepts us as Jesus, as his only Son, forever.

When the hour of death comes, we may not be conscious. It may come very suddenly, by reason of an accident, by reason of a heart attack; there are a million and one possibilities left to our imagination but this does not matter. The point is: *the surrender will have been made thousands of times!* The Father will understand that each of us had the power, which we exercised, the power, with his Son Jesus, to lay down our life freely, lovingly and definitively. Then there will be no obstacle to the consummation of our love. Life and holiness will be ours forever in the communion of the Most Blessed Trinity.

14. The Eucharist

"I Love the Father"—
"The Father Loves Me"

When we are speaking about the Eucharist, we speak about what the Second Vatican Council calls *"the source and summit of our Christian life."* We are speaking about the center of our faith and about the love of God that has made the Eucharist possible. I would like to begin by turning our thoughts to the words of Jesus in the fourteenth chapter of St. John's Gospel. Jesus says: "If you loved me, you would rejoice that I am going to the Father....the world must know that I love the Father and that I do just as the Father has commanded me. Get up, let us go" (John 14:28, 31).

These words express the great revelation that *Jesus loves his Father*. And in another place Jesus will tell us clearly that *the Father loves the Son*, the Father loves him. But these words also tell us that Jesus wants the world to know that he fulfills the Father's will. And because he fulfills the Father's will, he tells his apostles: "Come, then! Let us be on our way." Let us also be on our way to celebrate the sacrifice of the cross, to celebrate the Eucharist.

The Eucharist:
Mystery of Trinitarian Love

There are many profound reasons why Jesus died. There are many profound reasons why he offered up the Eucharist as a memorial of his death on Calvary. Jesus died for his church. In a special way Jesus died for his Mother. But above all, *Jesus died because he loved his Father*. He died to fulfill the will of his Father. In other words: "...the world must know that I love the Father and do as the Father has commanded me. Come, then! Let us be on our way."

I am suggesting that the key to understanding the Eucharist in its most profound dimension is to understand that Jesus went to his death motivated by a great love for his Father. The Eucharist *is* indeed the mystery of Christ's love and above all it is the mystery of Christ's love for his Father.

Some years ago a book came out entitled, *Gift and Mystery*. It was the short autobiography of Pope John Paul II that he presented to the world on the occasion of the fiftieth anniversary of his ordination to the priesthood. And in that book he recounts what he had previously said on the occasion of an interview with one of the journalists who accompanied him on one of his pastoral visits around the world. The interview went something like this.

"Holy Father, as pope you must have many problems, but also as pope there must be many joys in your life. Tell us what your greatest joy is." And the pope answered that *the greatest joy* that he has as pope is to be able, like every Catholic priest, *to celebrate the Eucharist every day*.

These words show the depth of his faith in the eucharistic mystery; they show the depth of his love for the sacrifice of the Mass. Over many years he has meditated on the Eucharist. And I would suggest now, together with Jesus and John Paul II: "Let us be on our way"—on our way to enter the great mystery of God's love.

The origin of the Eucharist is *the Last Supper* and *the sacrifice of Calvary*—both of which are commemorated and reenacted in the Eucharist, both of which are different moments in the one salvific reality of Christ's paschal mystery. But if we are to understand this life-giving event proclaimed at the Last Supper and enacted in immolation on Calvary, we must go back to what we have been speaking about: to the relation of Jesus with his Father—in other words to the Most Blessed Trinity.

Here we find the deepest explanation of the Most Blessed Sacrament—the deepest explanation of the Mass. The Council of Trent, over four hundred years ago, defined the Mass as a true sacrifice that recalls and renews Christ's immolation on Calvary. But why did Christ give himself over to death on Calvary? Why does he give himself in the Eucharist? Here of course we must speak of sin and redemption, of Christ's desire to save the world from sin and to communicate his life to humanity. Here we must speak of God's love for humanity, just as St. John does: "For God so loved the world that he gave his only Son, so that everyone who believes in him might not perish but might have eternal life. For God did not send the Son into the world to condemn the world, but that the world might be saved through him" (John 3:16–17).

This is a stupendous revelation that explains the Eucharist—*the love of God for us, the love of the Father in sending his Son to redeem the world*. But there are *two other aspects of God's love* that are even more stupendous and basic, without which we will not understand the Eucharist and all the suffering that Christ endured on Calvary.

The Eucharist flows directly from the love of the Son of God for his Father, in response to the eternal love by which he is loved by the Father in the Holy Spirit.

The Second Vatican Council tells us that the Eucharist contains all the riches of the Church (cf. *Presbyterorum Ordinis*, 5), and that it is the source and summit of all Christian life. Why? Because the love of the Father, the Son and the Holy Spirit is directly involved.

Jesus took great pleasure in proclaiming to the world—it was his greatest proclamation—*the love that the Father has for him* and the love that he has for the Father. These, I would dare say, are the most sublime words of divine revelation:

"The Father loves the Son" (John 3:35; 5:20).

"The Father loves me" (John 10:17).

"I love the Father" (John 14:31).

Jesus' Sacrifice and the Father's Acceptance

Regarding this last revelation—"I love the Father"—what is the context? We have already seen it at the beginning of this reflection. *Jesus is ready* to go to his hour. The prince of this world is at hand. He has no hold on Jesus. The world must know that he loves the Father. And therefore he says: "Come, then! Let us be on our way."

And so Jesus goes forth to Calvary, to death and immolation. There is an explicit connection between Calvary and Christ's loving his Father. In other words, Calvary is motivated by his love for the Father and his obedience to the Father. Calvary—with Jesus hanging on the Cross—is the divine plan of the Father for the redemption of the world. *Calvary*, and therefore the Eucharist, is *the trinitarian response to sin.* But it remains *the exchange of love between the Father and the Son in the Holy Spirit.*

This exchange of love is so great, the Son's acceptance of death is so full of love, that the Father wants the world to know of his acceptance. *The Father's response of love is the resurrection of his Son.* This is the meaning of Easter. *The Father raises the sacred humanity of Jesus to life in order* to confirm the redemption of the world and *to proclaim his eternal love for his Son,* his acceptance of the obedience of the Son, his acceptance of the sacrifice.

Saint Paul tells us in his Letter to the Philippians, in speaking of Christ, that "he humbled himself, / becoming obedient to death, / even death on a cross. / Because of this, God greatly exalted him / and bestowed on him the name / that is above every name, / that at the name of Jesus / every knee should bend, / of those in heaven and on earth and under the earth, / and every tongue confess that / Jesus Christ is Lord, / to the glory of the Father" (Phil 2:8–11). All of this shows us how profound the mystery of redemption; how great Christ's love for his Father; how fruitful Christ's obedience; how glorious the Father's acceptance of the sacrifice, his ratification of Christ's death by raising him to life! With St. Paul, we exclaim: "Oh, the depth of the riches and wisdom and knowledge of God!" (Rom 11:33).

The Sacrifice and Worship of the Community

In the exchange of love between Jesus and his Father we see explained the great mystery of the sacrifice of Calvary, even as it is anticipated at the Last Supper. We also note that the sacrifice of the infinite divine love of Christ becomes, by God's loving design in the Eucharist, *the sacrifice of the church*, our sacrifice.

As the sacrifice of Christ and his church, the Eucharist is our worship and we are privileged to partake in the eucharistic sacrifice every day of our lives. We are privileged to be able to do this as a community, to offer God praise as foreshadowed in the Old Testament, in the great assembly.

Let us never forget that the offering of the church's sacrifice is a great hymn of praise, thanksgiving, adoration, reparation and supplication on the part of the entire assembly. *We are in this together.*

Sent Forth to Adore and to Serve

At the end of Mass we are sent forth in order to serve in the name of Jesus. We are sent out from the Eucharist in order that, by the power of the Eucharist, we may contribute to the building up of the body of Christ.

As soon as we go out, our thought is to come back; to come back to the Eucharist at the time appointed by Christ. In the meantime we profess the eucharistic faith of the church as expressed throughout the centuries. The liturgy that we have celebrated as an act of adoration—as the Second Vatican Council calls it: "the worship of divine majesty"—is prolonged in *adoration of the Blessed Sacrament*, the real presence of Christ in our midst.

We believe and we proclaim the faith of the church that, after the celebration of the Eucharist, Jesus himself remains in the Blessed Sacrament in his glorified flesh, in his glorified humanity, to be adored and loved and to be a permanent source of union and life. And to the Blessed Sacrament present on the altar, the Catholic Church attributes *latria*, which is *the adoration that is owing only to the living God*. And this Eucharist, which contains all the treasures of the church and is "the primary and indispensable source from which the faithful are to derive the true Christian spirit" (*Sacrosanctum Concilium*, 14), is at one and the same time a *sacrifice*, a *banquet* and *the sacred presence of the Lord Jesus*. And the sacred eucharistic presence of the Lord, whom we adore, constantly directs our hearts back to the celebration in the assembly when once again we will all be together in order to renew the eucharistic celebration and to be sent out once again on our mission to the world.

This mission to the world takes its origin from the Eucharist and receives its dynamism from the Eucharist to embrace charity and service in the church.

We have seen in the history of the church not only people like Pope John Paul II with an immense love of the Eucharist, but we have also seen the martyrs, the imprisoned confessors, the holy virgins and Religious who have understood the Eucharist and have been willing to give everything in order to participate in the celebration and in order to possess the sacramental presence of Christ. The saints and heroes of our church have given us an example of *the effort that we must expend in order to participate in the Eucharist*, in order to adore Christ's presence in the Blessed Sacrament. Millions of holy lay people and Religious in the church, over the centuries, have made supreme efforts to demonstrate their faith in the Eucharist and to avail themselves, amidst difficulties and tribulations, of the eucharistic celebration and of eucharistic adoration.

The Eucharist is undoubtedly the center of our life, because Jesus is the center of our life, just as he is the object of the Father's eternal complacency—the Father's eternal love.

In our prayer let us not forget the importance of passing part of our time with Jesus in the Blessed Sacrament. Although we may need a certain freedom in choosing a comfortable place to pray, let us realize how important it is for us to keep Jesus company.

In 1997, in the Synod of Bishops for America, it was my privilege to be a participant and my privilege to speak. The topic of my intervention was *prayer*. I mentioned at the time that it is my conviction and the conviction of other bishops throughout the world that there is *a new emerging sign of the times* and it is *eucharistic adoration*.

Powerful Incentive and Challenge to Service

There are many indications in the world that God wishes to draw further attention to his beloved Son present in the Eucharist. There are many indications that eucharistic adoration is a form of prayer particularly adapted to this present moment. It is a particular form of manifesting faith in the total mystery of the Eucharist, which is sacrifice and banquet, sacred presence and viaticum. Eucharistic adoration is a powerful incentive and challenge to ever more generous service to those in need.

The Second Vatican Council has been an enormous grace in the life of the church, particularly in emphasizing over and over again the role of the Christian people as a eucharistic people. There have been some aberrations of interpretation of the Second Vatican Council. There have been some exaggerations and misinterpretations of the church's teaching on the Eucharist. Many of these difficulties have now passed. It is time to get on in the life of the church with traditional eucharistic piety as enriched and explained and exalted by the Second Vatican Council and the postconciliar implementation of the popes.

I cannot overemphasize the importance of *the community's full, conscious and active participation in the eucharistic sacrifice!* I cannot overemphasize the importance of the graces that are received for the living and the dead by this internal and external participation of all the members of the church in the eucharistic assembly. I cannot overemphasize the importance of prayer before the Blessed Sacrament, of eucharistic adoration, eucharistic exposition, the eucharistic holy hour, visits to the Blessed Sacrament and the renewal of our own faith, day in and day out, in the words of Jesus who says: "For my flesh is true food, and my blood is true drink. Whoever eats my flesh and drinks my blood remains in me and I in him. Just as the living Father sent me and I have life because of the Father, so also the one who feeds on me will have life because of me" (John 6:55–57).

There is much more that we could say about participation in the Eucharist, about external reverence, about the internal dispositions that we bring to the Eucharist, about our community singing and about the dignity of every form of eucharistic participation and ministry. Let us remember that our Holy Father set the year 2000 as the great eucharistic year. This emphasis in the life of the church *urges us* to be faithful, to grow in the love of the Eucharist so as to be an ever more fervent eucharistic community committed to the service of the world.

We have a goal to reach and it is all for the glory of the Father. Our eucharistic journey beckons us. Jesus is with us to lead us on. He says to us: "Come, then! Let us be on our way." And our response to him is: *Jesus, I trust in you!*

15. Chosen by the Father, Chosen by Christ

A very wonderful aspect of our lives is *the choice that God has made of us for his purposes.* A number of the texts of sacred scripture speak to us about this mystery of God's choice. So very worthy of reflection is the beautiful text of St. Paul in his Letter to the Ephesians, which speaks of our fundamental voca- tion: "Blessed be the God and Father of our Lord Jesus Christ, who has blessed us in Christ with every spiritual blessing in the heavens, as he chose us in him, before the foundation of the world, to be holy and without blemish before him. In love he destined us for adoption to himself through Jesus Christ, in accord with the favor of his will, for the praise of the glory of his grace that he granted us in the beloved" (Eph 1:3–6).

The Father's Plan

This text invites us to the praise of God for the fact that *the Father has chosen us from all eternity in Jesus.* We are indeed chosen in Jesus. We see what a loving choice God has made; how he has lavished us with benefits. We have been chosen to be holy and without blemish. We are talking here about our vocation to divine adoption and at the same time we are talking about our vocation to Christian holiness, and all of this means we have indeed been chosen by the Father in Christ.

From verse six it is clearly evident that God has destined us for the praise of the glory of his grace which he has granted us in his beloved Son. We are reminded right away that, through Christ, God's grace has triumphed in us and we must praise what God has accomplished. If God has chosen us to be his sons and daughters in his beloved Son, if he has chosen us to be holy and without blemish, it is so that we may attain all of this through Christ, and so that our lives may acknowledge the glory, the wonderful efficacy of grace, which makes all of this possible.

Saint Paul wants us to join in with him in blessing the God and Father of our Lord Jesus Christ for the choice that he has freely made of us in his Eternal Word. This choice is what Paul means by saying that we have been "*predestined.*" We are indeed blessed because God has chosen us as his own. In the words of Psalm 33: "Happy the nation whose God is the LORD, / the people chosen as his very own" (v. 12).

Friendship with Jesus

Besides the call to divine adoption and to holiness, Jesus points out at the Last Supper *the call of his disciples to friendship with himself.* The text is very beautiful: "I have called you friends, because I have told you everything I have heard from my Father. It was not you who chose me, but I who chose you and appointed you to go and bear fruit that will remain, so that whatever you ask the Father in my name he may give you. This I command you: love one another" (John 15:15–17).

Two elements of great importance for us as disciples are to know that we have been chosen to enjoy friendship with Christ and to bear fruit in our Christian lives. He explains to us the reason he calls us friends; it is that he has told us everything that he has heard from the Father. Our friendship with Christ brings us into trinitarian intimacy. Christ reveals the Father to us and in doing this he makes us his friends. At the same time he tells us: "It was...I who chose you and appointed you to go and bear fruit that will remain."

At different stages in our lives we may have questionings about the providence of God. I do not say "doubts" because many questionings do not make a doubt and many questionings do not destroy the trust that we have in Jesus when we frequently repeat to him: *Jesus, I trust in you!*

But over the years we can wonder why it is that God places us in a particular circumstance, why it is that he chose a particular mission or situation for us. Today we see that Jesus tells us: "It was I who chose you." And his choice is connected with the fact that our lives are destined for fruitfulness—to have an impact on the church.

When my mother died, I remember there was a card that she had in the bedroom. I wish I could find that card again. I wish I could somewhere discover the origin of what was written on it. All I remember, though, are the first lines and I would like so much to read once again the rest of the card. But the first lines went like this: "Never to look beyond me out of my little sphere. If I could fill another, God wouldn't keep me here."

What contentment there is in knowing that it was Christ who chose us. He chose us for a purpose. He chose us for a mission, for fruitfulness. And he maintains his choice and it is up to us to live in faith and trust.

Consecration and Mission

In the following verses of the fifteenth chapter of St. John's Gospel, Jesus explains to his disciples that they no longer belong to the world because his choice of them has drawn them out of the world. He even goes so far as to say that this choice of his causes the world to hate them.

How wonderful to think that we have been chosen by Christ, that *we have been chosen to be fruitful in our mission*—the duration of which he supervises. How sobering to realize the dramatic consequences of the choice that God has personally made of us and that he confirms by his providence.

You see where this leads us. It leads us to a point where there is *an absolute priority in our life of clinging to Christ*, of clinging to his word, of clinging to his church, of clinging to his mission and to our mission!

We cannot appease the world. We belong to Christ. We have been chosen by Christ.

The third chapter of St. Mark speaks to us about the choice of the twelve apostles. There are different elements in this text that apply only to the Twelve, but certainly there are extremely important elements that are characteristic of all the disciples of Jesus. In relating to us the choice of Jesus, St. Mark gives us a wonderful insight into the way that Jesus made his choice. Saint Mark's information is supplemented also by the information of St. Luke. Jesus went up the mountain and he passed the night in prayer. He summoned the men he himself had decided on and there were twelve of them. The basic choice that Jesus made of the Twelve was as follows: "He appointed twelve [whom he also named apostles] that they might be with him and he might send them forth..." (Mark 3:14).

The purpose of the choice of the apostles, which is common to all the disciples of Jesus in the first generation and up until now, is that they were chosen for the double aspect: *to be with him* and *to be sent forth*. How essential it was for the apostles to be with Jesus. The 1970 *New American Bible* says "as his companions" and this too is a beautiful phrase.

When Jesus chooses his followers, *companionship with him is part of the gift that he gives*. He calls them to be with him or to be his companions precisely because he reserves for them a mission. And this is, dear friends, your calling. This is the choice that Jesus has made of you: to be his companions and then to be sent forth.

To Choose to Respond

As we reflect on God's choice of us, we also realize that at a given moment we too are called to choose, *to choose to respond to him* in different ways; to respond to him freely; to respond to him lovingly; to respond to him courageously. In the Gospel of St. Luke, Jesus praises the choice that Mary of Bethany made, how she, chosen by him, then chose to adhere to him in prayer. Jesus says: "Mary has chosen the better part and it will not be taken from her" (Luke 10:42).

God's choice in no way takes away our freedom. It is rather an incentive for us to choose him in return. In his First Letter to the Corinthians St. Paul establishes a principle of extreme importance in regard to the choice God makes of us. He tells us that the choice belongs to God and so does the glory. Let us listen to these magnificent words: "Consider your own calling, brothers. Not many of you were wise by human standards, not many were powerful, not many were of noble birth. Rather, God chose the foolish of the world to shame the wise, and God chose the weak of the world to shame the strong, and God chose the lowly and despised of the world, those who count for nothing, to reduce to nothing those who are something, so that no human being might boast before God. It is due to him that you are in Christ Jesus, who became for us wisdom from God, as well as righteousness, sanctification, and redemption, so that, as it is written, 'Whoever boasts, should boast in the Lord'" (1 Cor 1:26–31).

God's Freedom Challenges Our Freedom

What emerges from this text of St. Paul is that we have *no right to be chosen*, either by Jesus or by the Father in Jesus. But if God chooses us, and he does, then our weakness and our limitations do not restrict his action and the power of his working in us.

Saint James expands the text of St. Paul to the Corinthians when he says: "Did not God choose those who are poor in the world to be rich in faith and heirs of the kingdom that he promised to those who love him?" (Jas 2:5). So often we find that the very poor in so many ways are indeed chosen by God to be rich in faith and heirs of the kingdom. In this context, St. James gives us a very sobering lesson in regard to our attitude toward the poor.

There is no doubt that the choice is made by God. God chooses whom he wills. He chooses us for his purpose. He creates us and redeems us without our collaboration, but he will not save us—and he does not desire to save the world—without our collaboration. And so he asks us constantly *to accept his choice, to respond to this choice*, to open ourselves to holiness.

In the sixth chapter of St. John's Gospel we see in the discourse on the Eucharist how Jesus became a sign of contradiction to the world. And many of the disciples, who had been chosen by him, returned to their former way of life and no longer accompanied him. At that point Jesus said to the Twelve: "Do you also want to leave?" (John 6:67). And Peter answered him saying: "Master, to whom shall we go? You have the words of eternal life. We have come to believe and are convinced that you are the Holy One of God" (vv. 68–69). Then Jesus answered them saying: "Did I not choose you twelve? Yet is not one of you a devil?" (v. 70). And St. John goes on to say that he was talking about Judas Iscariot who was to betray him.

Throughout all the scriptures we see how the choice that God makes of his servants is regulated by *his sovereign freedom*. But, nevertheless, those who are chosen are invited, indeed required, to exercise their freedom in order to ratify the choice that has been made of them by Jesus and in Jesus.

There is much to be said about baptismal consecration, but basically it is such a wonderful opportunity to surrender ourselves to the God who chose us. In order to belong totally to him, in order to be totally at his disposal, the various aspects of our life give us the occasion to ratify the choice that God has made of us in Christ, to ratify the choice that Christ has made of us to associate us in his mission. Our ratification must always lead us back to the Eucharist. It must always lead us to the praise of God in union with Christ; it must always lead us to praise the glory of his grace through which we are able to accomplish the role for which we were chosen. "Blessed be the God and Father of our Lord Jesus Christ, who has blessed us in Christ with every spiritual blessing in the heavens" (Eph 1:3).

16. Readiness
to Ask Forgiveness
and to Forgive Others

Insisting On God's Mercy!

We remember the great works that the Lord has accomplished through all his holy saints. Actually the saints themselves are among the works of the Lord, which the Psalms tell us not to forget: "Do not forget the works of the Lord!" (cf. Ps 78:7).

These words are especially meaningful to me, because they are part of the injunction that Pope John Paul II gave me the day he ordained me a bishop on the feast of the Triumph of the Holy Cross back in 1985. These words were the responsory of that feast.

All of us are challenged by these words. And *among the great works of God in our lives is the gift of his forgiveness*, his pardon, his compassion, his consolation. Whoever reads the encyclical of Pope John Paul II *Dives in Misericordia* ("Rich in Mercy") will understand *why the church insists on God's mercy*. I have already reflected on it at some length, but the gospel requires us to return to this topic again and again.

One day, Peter had a question for Jesus: "How often must I forgive my brother when he wrongs me?" The answer is so very clear: *we must forgive over and over again.* It is like the forgiveness that God gives us: there is no end to it. Hence we have the formula: "seventy times seven," or in the revised *New American Bible*, which is used in the new *Lectionary*: "seventy-seven times." These two interpretations are possible, but Christ's intention is equally clear in the text.

Mercy Requires Mercy

After this, Jesus tells the story of how the king treated his servant. The king was moved with pity, forgave him his debt and let him go. The king showed great mercy.

But then what happens? The man refused to forgive his fellow servant; he showed no mercy. The king was angry. The words that Jesus cites echo down the centuries: "Should you not have had pity on your fellow servant, as I had pity on you?" (Matt 18:33).

We have many weaknesses, which God understands and even transforms, but *a lack of mercy on our part stirs up the anger of God*, precisely because he has been so merciful and forgiving toward us.

Even as we strive not to forget the works of the Lord—including especially his mercy in our lives—we open our hearts to offer mercy and to receive it ever more abundantly.

God is listening to our prayer, expressed many times a day: "Forgive us our trespasses as we forgive those who trespass against us."

And then once again: how wonderful is the sacrament of penance, the sacrament of reconciliation, the sacrament of confession in which we meet personally a forgiving and merciful Lord who repeatedly gives us the opportunity to say to him: *Jesus, I trust in you!*

We gratefully receive his redeeming and healing love in the Eucharist each day. Our readiness to ask forgiveness and to forgive others makes us appreciate the sacrament of penance and receive it frequently.

Our Blessed Mother's words fill us with joy: "His mercy is from age to age / to those who fear him" (Luke 1:50).

17. Prayer

Any Call to Action Is First of All a Call to Prayer

Prayer is a dialogue of love. In a special way I would like to recommend part four of the *Catechism of the Catholic Church*. It is indeed a beautiful presentation on Christian prayer.

Let me begin by quoting Saint Thérèse's answer to the first question of part four: What is prayer? Saint Thérèse of Lisieux says: "For me, prayer is a surge of the heart; it is a simple look turned toward heaven, it is a cry of recognition and of love, embracing both trial and joy."

These are certainly beautiful elements in prayer: *a surge of the heart, a simple look, a cry of recognition and of love*. And the *Catechism* will complete all those elements, with even more Christocentric and trinitarian elements from the tradition of the church.

Charism of Prayer

On my part, I would like to make reference in the context of prayer to both Pope Paul VI and Pope John Paul II.

In 1976, there was a large meeting in Detroit. It was entitled: "A Call to Action." The purpose of this meeting was to sensitize the church in the United States to the social doctrine of the church, to the exigencies of justice and to the requirements of human dignity in the world. The aim was altogether laudatory.

A special message was asked of Pope Paul VI. He consented and sent a message to the gathering. In the course of that message, as he encouraged the people to take their responsibility in regard to the social teaching of the church, he also made this statement: "In the long tradition of the Church any call to action is first of all a call to prayer." History will judge the outcome of the "Call to Action" as it has subsequently developed in the United States. But history will also judge and vindicate Pope Paul VI in his insistence that *any call to action is first of all a call to prayer*.

This is the way Jesus has set up his church. This is the way Jesus has formulated the priorities of his church.

My second reference is to Pope John Paul II. I remember being with him on one of his pastoral visits in Africa. The Holy Father had come to the end of a very long day. He had fulfilled all his obligations. He had finished all his meetings. Dinner was over. There were yet people to greet and to thank, and finally the time came when he could sit down in a chair and say that the day was over.

I had the great pleasure at the time of spending a few moments with him together with a Polish colleague of mine. The three of us sat in a nunciature in Africa and spoke briefly about the blessings of the day. All of us were extremely tired. At a given moment, the Holy Father rose, went into the chapel. My colleague and I remained outside as the pope withdrew for private prayer. Five minutes, ten minutes, fifteen minutes, twenty minutes—whatever it was passed by. And then the pope came back again. This time he was visibly refreshed. *He had been with Christ in prayer*. He had found the joy that he finds every day before the Blessed Sacrament. He was renewed physically, spiritually, in every way through his dialogue of love with Christ.

It is no secret to the world that a great deal of the success of the pontificate of John Paul II is due to his prayer. God has undoubtedly given to him as to Paul Paul VI *a great charism of prayer*: sustained prayer, joyful prayer, fruitful prayer.

Example of Jesus and Mary

The popes give us an excellent example, but they themselves draw on the example of Jesus. It is Jesus who has taught the church the great lesson of prayer. We know that Jesus prayed before his major decisions. We know that he prayed before the extremely important decision of choosing his twelve apostles. Saint Luke reminds us: "In those days he departed to the mountain to pray, and he spent the night in prayer to God. When day came, he called his disciples to himself, and from them he chose Twelve, whom he also named apostles..." (Luke 6:12–13).

Jesus found delight in conversing with his Father. He submitted to him his pastoral decisions. He received strength for his human nature from the prayer that he offered to his Father. In the garden of Gethsemane, when Jesus was in his agony, he prayed more earnestly, so fervently that his sweat became like drops of blood falling on the ground (cf. Luke 22:45).

The church rejoices also in the example of Mary. We know that she lived in union with God. We know that she drew strength from prayer, strength that would permit her to submit to God's great salvific plan and to declare herself the humble servant of the Lord.

We remember, too, the great novena she made for nine months. We can only imagine the fervor with which she prayed during her pregnancy as she adored the Incarnate Word of God present in her womb.

We have spoken about Christ's call to conversion and now we must also mention Christ's call to prayer. Jesus tells us: "Be vigilant at all times and pray that you have the strength to escape the tribulations that are imminent and to stand before the Son of Man" (Luke 21:36).

Not only did Jesus encourage us to pray, but *Jesus taught us to pray*. And He taught us to pray the Our Father. He meticulously told us how to address God. He told us what to ask for and how to do it. Jesus is the master of our prayer. We know that prayer places everything in perspective. Prayer is extremely necessary in order to be able to read the signs of the times and interpret them correctly.

How important it is for Religious to pray; how important it is for them to discern the signs of the times; to discern correctly all that touches their lives and their apostolates.

In prayer we all discover the needs of our brothers and sisters. In prayer we realize what is necessary for the world and what is necessary for us to do, in order to serve the world.

Prayer is a source of joy. Religious without joy are an anomaly. There is no justification for religious life that does not give the witness of joyful renunciation, joyful love, the joyful apostolate.

In prayer the word of God presented to us in the scriptures is understood, applied and lived. At the same time *the sacred scriptures are the inspiration for our prayer*. Prayer is the opportunity for us to turn to the word of God and, with total and complete openness in the Holy Spirit and in the church, to draw forth the treasures that God has placed at our disposal.

A Praying Community

The church is a praying community. The church was founded in order to pray. Every local parish, every local church exists in order to be an assembly of prayer. Every religious congregation in the church is and must always be a community of prayer. We remember the prophetic words of Pope Paul VI in his apostolic exhortation *Evangelica Testificatio*. At that time he spoke about the fervor of prayer in a congregation as being decisive in whether it would survive:

"Do not forget the witness of history: faithfulness to prayer or its abandonment is the test of the vitality or decadence of the religious life" (No. 42).

Prayer is needed in the church in order *to cope with suffering*. It was the only way that Jesus had to cope with his suffering; it is the only way that we can cope with ours. It is also necessary in order to be able *to cope with sin and the effects of sin*. It is in prayer that *we confront temptations* to sin and the effects of sin in our own lives and in our community. In prayer we reject any lack of trust that surfaces in our heart when we say: *Jesus, I trust in you!*

Partners in Intercession

We know that Jesus attributed great importance to his own role as intercessor with the Father. We know that the Holy Spirit intercedes for the church. We know that the church is called upon to intercede for the world. *The task of intercession* is one of the great obligations of the church.

Saint Paul highlights the intercessory role, both of the Holy Spirit and of Jesus. He says: "The Spirit too comes to the aid of our weakness; for we do not know how to pray as we ought, but the Spirit himself intercedes with inexpressible groanings. And the one who searches hearts knows what is the intention of the Spirit, because it intercedes for the holy ones according to God's will" (Rom 8:26–27). Saint Paul then draws attention to the role of Christ saying: "If God is for us, who can be against us?...Who will condemn? It is Christ [Jesus] who died, rather, was raised, who also is at the right hand of God, who indeed intercedes for us" (Rom 8:31, 34).

In the church there is a need for the prayer of intercession to go on day and night for the living and for the dead. The Holy Spirit and Christ seek partners in their intercession and are willing to bestow this tremendous grace. Saint Paul in his First Letter to Timothy says: "First of all, then, I ask that supplications, prayers, petitions, and thanksgivings be offered for everyone" (1 Tim 2:1). This concept of intercession is one that is extremely valuable as we pray the breviary, as we pray the prayer of the church and engage with Christ and the Holy Spirit in their mission of interceding for the world.

The author of the Letter to the Hebrews emphasizes how *Christ's mission of intercession is linked to his mission of salvation.* He says, referring to Christ: "Therefore, he is always able to save those who approach God through him, since he lives forever to make intercession for them" (Heb 7:25).

Is not this one of our special roles? Is this not a very wonderful part of our Christian mission to live with Christ and the Holy Spirit in intercession? To live with Christ interceding always for the church and for the world? To be united with the Spirit of God's love, interceding with the Spirit for the church and the salvation of the world?

Liturgical Prayer and Personal Piety

So much a part of the church's prayer life is linked to the Liturgy of the Hours. So much of the success of our prayer depends on the way that we offer up the prayer of praise which is the divine office. We are called to join in the praise of God at the different hours of our day. We are also called, as we praise the Father in union with Jesus, to intercede for all those who need salvation and eternal life.

I have already mentioned that the liturgy is described by the Second Vatican Council as the worship of the divine majesty. Liturgical prayer, which includes not only the Eucharist, but also the celebration of the sacraments and the divine office or the Liturgy of the Hours, is indeed prayer par excellence. It is the prayer in which the bride of Christ speaks to the Spirit. It is the prayer in which Jesus the bridegroom of the church speaks to his Father. It is the prayer in which he presents to his Father the intercession of his church; this intercession is made one in the great act whereby he lives to intercede for us always.

Yet the Second Vatican Council tells us that liturgical prayer does not exhaust all the prayers of the church. The dignity of meditation and contemplation, the dignity of simple individual prayer, the dignity of community prayer—all this remains very much intact after the Second Vatican Council.

We know with what predilection the Holy Father invokes our Blessed Mother. We know how the saints have found joy and consolation and inspiration in the rosary. We know how the various devotions in the church have been occasions of grace for millions of faithful people over the years.

Eucharistic Adoration

Above all we realize how eucharistic adoration, of which I have already spoken, is such an effective means of interceding with the Father in the name of Jesus. It is such a wonderful practice that the faith and piety of the church over the years have preserved for us and encouraged us to utilize.

If there is something that I would leave as *a legacy of this reflection*, it would be to recommend *frequent adoration of Jesus in the Blessed Sacrament*. It would be to explore the secrets of his sacred heart and his merciful love through adoration of the Blessed Sacrament and at the same time be brought back again to the eucharistic celebration, in which the assembly offers official praise to God through Christ.

In regard to the legacy of encouraging eucharistic adoration, I would also suggest that Christ himself speaks to us at that time and shares with us the desires of his heart for his church, for those in need, his desire to fill all people with his grace, to convert sinful hearts and to fortify the clergy, Religious and laity of the church.

But since eucharistic adoration brings us into contact with the merciful Christ and his desire to spread mercy in his church, I would likewise suggest that he speaks to us about the sacrament of mercy, about the sacrament of penance in our lives.

Invoking the Father

One last word! Let us remember that as we study the exquisite formulas of Christian prayer, all of which have been introduced into the church through the inspiration of the Holy Spirit, and all of which correspond to one or another need in the church, we will never find a more perfect formula than that taught to the apostles by Jesus himself: the Our Father.

There can never be a more intimate moment in our relationship with God than when, entering into the person of Jesus Christ, entering into his sentiments, exulting in our relationship to the Father and invoking our adoption in Christ Jesus, we address God *as Father*. At the very end of our lives, as we reach the last prayer that we have to say, we will certainly want to *proclaim the name of Jesus*. He will have been for our entire life, the way, the truth and the life for us. But as we prepare in our last moment for heavenly glory in the person of Jesus we will once again want to *invoke the Father*.

All Christian life is a journey to the Father, in union with Christ and in the Holy Spirit. When we are finally configured definitively to Christ Jesus, there will be only one invocation to make and that will be in the communion of the Most Blessed Trinity. *With Jesus we shall invoke the Father*.

18. Freedom and Holiness

Without multiplying words on the day he died on the cross, Christ showed us *the meaning of freedom and holiness.* He died because he willed freely to do so, because he willed freely to fulfill the Father's will. To be able to do the Father's will freely is *true freedom;* to actually do it is *holiness.* Christ was able to do it and he did it. Christ was free, and from his freedom there shone forth the holiness of his humanity.

In the gospel we will hear Jesus speaking to his disciples and saying: "There is a baptism with which I must be baptized, and how great is my anguish until it is accomplished!" (Luke 12:50).

Christ's Surrender on Calvary

Let us go for a moment to Calvary, where indeed it is over. What a magnificent scene we have on Calvary as Christ dies. Absolutely everything is accomplished. The prophecies are fulfilled. God's plan is perfectly on course. Jesus has now spoken to his Father and to his Mother.

In speaking to his Father he has changed the words of scripture, availing himself of his sovereign right as God. He has quoted Psalm 36 but has willed to substitute the word *Father* where the context speaks of *Lord* and *faithful God* (cf. vv. 2, 6). And so he says:

"Father, into your hands I commend my spirit" (Luke 23:46).

In speaking to his Mother he declares her to be the Mother of his church. But he also attributes to her the title *woman*. It is the title of Genesis; it is the title that we find in the Book of Revelation. From this day forward Mary is declared to be *the woman of all salvation history.*

At this moment there is just one more act to accomplish. It is a very important one. Jesus intends to bow his head. It is the last outward sign of love for his Father. And then, and only then, Jesus gives up his spirit. The bowing of his head is the supreme outward act of his obedience to his Father. He then wills to die at the moment preordained by his Father. His life does not ebb away. His head does not fall in death. He bows his head; he surrenders his life. And we remember what he said as the good shepherd in the tenth chapter of St. John's Gospel: "A good shepherd lays down his life for the sheep.... I am the good shepherd...and I will lay down my life for the sheep.... This is why the Father loves me, because I lay down my life in order to take it up again. No one takes it from me, but I lay it down on my own. I have power to lay it down, and power to take it up again. This command I have received from my Father" (John 10:11, 14–15, 17–18). Jesus bows his head to assert his power and to proclaim loving obedience to the command of his Father.

It all happened as was foretold in the fifty-third chapter of Isaiah. "But the LORD laid upon him / the guilt of us all. / Though he was harshly treated, he submitted / and opened not his mouth; / Like a lamb led to the slaughter, / or a sheep before the shearers, / he was silent and opened not his mouth. / Oppressed and condemned he was taken away, / and who would have thought any more of his destiny?... / Because of his affliction / he shall see the light in fullness of days; / Through his suffering, my servant shall justify many, / and their guilt he shall bear. / Therefore I will give him his portion among the great, / and he shall divide the spoils with the mighty, / Because he surrendered himself to death / and was counted among the wicked; / And he shall take away the sins of many, / and win pardon for their offenses" (Isa 53:6–8, 11–12). Bowing his head Jesus exercised *the great power of his freedom.*

The Father's Acceptance

There is yet another phase of Christ's freedom: *the solemn recognition and ratification of Christ's freedom by the Father.* First of all, this recognition and ratification was signified as the curtain in the sanctuary was torn from top to bottom. "The earth quaked, rocks were split, tombs were opened, and the bodies of many saints who had fallen asleep were raised" (Matt 27:51–52). But all of this was nothing compared with the action of the Eternal Father who raised Jesus Christ from the dead on Easter Sunday.

The Father's action is the supreme acceptance of Jesus' freedom, in which the humanity of the risen one is confirmed in newness of life. In a special way, the church calls the resurrection of Jesus holy, because holiness is possible only with freedom. The total freedom of Jesus in his human nature has been exalted by the Father. In his risen humanity, as St. Paul explains, Jesus "lives for God." His sacred humanity after the resurrection is *the perfect expression of total and free adherence to God.*

Jesus is the example for the church of all freedom, and of all holiness made possible by freedom.

Our Blessed Mother Mary, as a creature of God, totally exemplifies freedom. She lived the truth of her relationship with God. She gave everything. She surrendered her will. Her testament of freedom is left to the world in her words: "Be it done unto me according to your word." And just as the ratification of Jesus' freedom is the resurrection, the ratification of Mary's freedom is the incarnation: "The word became flesh and dwelt among us" because the Virgin Mary accepted God's plan *with total surrender.*

We have a beautiful example of freedom in the feast of St. Maximilian Mary Kolbe! With what tremendous spiritual freedom he surrendered his life out of love, and, yes, because of hatred on the part of others for the church and her teaching that proclaims the dignity of every man, woman and child— of every person who shares humanity with the one who is the Son of God and the Son of Mary.

And then there is the question of freedom and holiness for all of us in the church. We know that there can be no holiness without freedom, and we know that *we cannot be free unless we live in truth—* the truth of our relationship with God and with one another. Only if we accept the gift of God's truth can we know his gift of freedom and in that freedom find holiness. The words of Jesus are so important for us: "If you remain in my word, you will truly be my disciples, and you will know the truth, and the truth will set you free" (John 8:31–32).

Jesus was then asked: "How can you say, 'You will become free'?" He answered them: "Amen, amen, I say to you, everyone who commits sin is a slave of sin" (vv. 33–34). Then he added: "...if a son frees you, then you will truly be free" (v. 36). If we trust the Son, He will free us more and more. *Jesus, I trust in you!*

Freedom Offered to God

The Lord Jesus is offering today to increase our freedom, to sanctify the freedom that he has already given us by his free gift of surrender on the cross. Let us remember that *Christ's gift to us is also our gift to him and to his Father and the Holy Spirit.* In freely obeying the Father's will, Mary gave humanity to the Son of God, becoming his Mother, and becoming the temple and spouse of the Holy Spirit. Like Mary, we can give back to God—Father, Son and Holy Spirit —our magnificent gift of freedom. We can say *yes* freely, over and over again: in joy and sorrow, in pain and anguish, in hope and peace.

Without our repeated *yes*, there is no spiritual fecundity, no possibility of doing great things for God, because God wants, above all, *to possess us* at the core of our being, which is the realm of our free-dom. He wants us to possess the physical freedom to be able to choose between good and evil, to choose him or to reject him, so that we may have the spiritual freedom always to say *yes* to him. "If a son frees you, then you will truly be free" (John 8:36).

Like Mary, we are called to nurture freedom in prayer, trying never to interrupt the response *yes* to the invitation of God. Freedom, obedience, holiness—all of these fuse, in the surrender of joy that we are called to make to Christ and his church.

In speaking of our life, we can say with Jesus: "No one takes it from me, but I lay it down on my own. I have power to lay it down..." (John 10:18).

19. *Evangelization*

The year 2000 was the twenty-fifth anniversary of the apostolic exhortation of Pope Paul VI, *Evangelii Nuntiandi*, issued on December 8, 1975. This document spelled out the great ideal of evangelization in the church. This document has been ratified and cited numerous times in the pontificate of Pope John Paul II, who has returned to this work of his predecessor Pope Paul VI on countless occasions.

Primary Importance of Witness of Life

During this reflection, I would like to touch on the overall evangelizing work of the church. One of the first values that Pope Paul VI proclaimed in describing evangelization is *the need for holiness*, the primary importance of witness of life. Pope Paul VI emphasizes the first means of evangelization as being the witness of an authentic Christian life given over to God and to one's neighbor. Even before issuing *Evangelii Nuntiandi* Pope Paul VI had stated: "Modern man listens more willingly to witnesses than to teachers, and if he does listen to teachers, it is because they are witnesses" (cf. *Evangelii Nuntiandi*, 41).

In the Gospel of St. John we have great interest shown by a group of Greeks at the time of the Passover. These Greeks had come to Jerusalem at the time of the feast. They were curious about Jesus. Saint John says: "They came to Philip, who was from Bethsaida in Galilee, and asked him, 'Sir, we would like to see Jesus'" (John 12:21). This event has a deep message for all of us who are involved in evangelization. The world is saying to us today: *we want to see Jesus!* And what is so impressive is that the world really does not want to see anyone else except Jesus. The world, for all its hostility, wants the authentic revelation of Jesus, despite the fact that his message leads to the cross.

In this episode we have a magnificent description of how our lives must present Jesus to the world and how our evangelizing methods must include that of witness and holiness of life. This gives us some indication of the dignity of being an evangelizer, the dignity of being involved in the world of evangelization. What dignity! What demands! What a challenge there is for the evangelizer—the evangelizer who is set upon communicating Christ and who is endeavoring, by evangelization, to fulfill the command of Christ: "Love one another as I love you" (John 15:12).

Deepest Identity of the Church

In reasserting our own dedication to evangelization, it is very important for us to understand what the church means by evangelization. The document *Evangelii Nuntiandi* helps us so much in this regard. The Holy Year 1975 was a year of magnificent documents. Another apostolic exhortation that had preceded *Evangelii Nuntiandi* by some weeks was entitled *Gaudete in Domino*. It is a beautiful treatise on Christian joy.

Pope Paul VI explained in great detail *the meaning of evangelization* and *the spirit of evangelization*. He captured the zeal of Jesus as evangelizer in the words recorded in St. Luke's Gospel where Jesus says: "I must proclaim the good news of the kingdom of God" (Luke 4:43).

Understanding Jesus' attitude toward evangelization, it is easier to understand the meaning of evangelization itself. All the different aspects of evangelization have been taken up by Pope Paul VI in his document, which is so useful for study and reflection.

Pope Paul VI made a special point of emphasizing *salvation* and *the kingdom of God*, as they relate to evangelization. As the kernel and center of his message, Christ proclaims salvation. Indeed, he proclaims a kingdom of salvation and these words—*kingdom* and *salvation*—are truly key words for Christ in enunciating the good news.

There are a number of very important points that are made in the apostolic exhortation, each of which furnishes a chapter for our meditation. One of these points concerns evangelization as *the vocation proper to the church*.

Let us listen to Pope Paul VI as he describes this aspect: "Evangelizing is, in fact, the grace and vocation proper to the Church, her deepest identity. She exists in order to evangelize, that is to say in order to preach and teach, to be the channel of the gift of

grace, to reconcile sinners with God and to perpetu-
ate Christ's sacrifice in the Mass, which is the memorial of his death and glorious resurrection" (*Evangelii
Nuntiandi*, 14).

But what is evangelization? What does evangelization involve? We remember once again that when
Jesus appeared on the scene for the first time as public evangelizer, he issued his call immediately—the
call to conversion. Yes, evangelization includes this
too. It is *a call to interior change*. It means bringing the
good news into all the strata of humanity and of
making humanity new.

A Clear Proclamation of the Lord Jesus

The church evangelizes, seeking to convert hearts.
But what else does evangelization involve? I have
already mentioned that it involves holiness of life
and genuine Christian witness. There are millions of
Christians who bear this witness in a wordless way
and, through the power of the Holy Spirit, stir up
irresistible questions in the hearts of those who see
how they live. There are many people who ask these
questions, and they ask them about us too: "Why are
these Christians like this?" "Why do they live in this
way?" "What or who is it that inspires them?" "Why
are they in our midst?" Remember God's question to
Elijah: "Why are you here?"

Such a witness is already a powerful proclamation
of the good news. All Christians are called to this
witness. Religious are called to it in a particular way.

Besides witness, however, there is also a need in our lives for *a clear and unequivocal proclamation of the Lord Jesus.*

Pope Paul VI has said this: "The good news proclaimed by the witness of life sooner or later has to be proclaimed by the word of life." But then he goes on to spell this out and say: "There is no true evangelization if the name, the teaching, the life, the promises, the Kingdom and the mystery of Jesus of Nazareth, the Son of God are not proclaimed" (*Evangelii Nuntiandi*, 22).

How important it is for us to ask ourselves: What is evangelization? What does it involve? What is its content? Here too Pope Paul VI has a memorable and succinct expression in reference to the content of evangelization. He says: "Evangelization will also contain—as the foundation, center and at the same time summit of its dynamism—a clear proclamation that in Jesus Christ the Son of God made man, who died and rose from the dead, salvation is offered to all men, as a gift of God's grace and mercy" (*ibid.*, 27). If Jesus gives salvation as a gift of mercy, he deserves to be invoked with trust: "*Jesus, I trust in you!*"

The Person to Be Evangelized

We know, therefore, that to evangelize is first of all to bear witness in a simple and direct way to God revealed by Jesus Christ, and in the Holy Spirit; to bear witness that, in his Son, God has loved the world. But we also know that evangelization would not be complete if it did not take into account the relationship that exists between the gospel and daily life. Pope Paul says: "This is why evangelization involves an explicit message, adapted to the different situations constantly being realized, about the rights and duties of every human being, about family life, without which personal growth and development is hardly possible, about life in society, about international life, peace, justice and development—a message especially energetic today about liberation" (*Evangelii Nuntiandi*, 29).

How, in fact, could the church proclaim Christ's new commandment of love and not be concerned with the daily life of her members, the daily life of all people? It is from our own zeal for evangelization that we derive zeal also for service. For example, the service that we endeavor to give to young people, the service that we endeavor to give to families, all in the name of Jesus and all part of his gospel message, ever striving to lead everyone to full participation in the kingdom of God and in salvation. We realize very clearly that the person to be evangelized is not an abstract being, but is subject to social, economic, political, cultural and religious factors.

The church is more than ready to embrace the whole area of human advancement, which includes development and liberation, seeing therein profound links with evangelization. The church takes her example from Jesus who went about doing good, from Jesus who healed the sick, who came to give his life as a ransom for many, Jesus who came to serve and not to be served.

The church is never willing to disassociate herself from the temporal problems of the world. Her missionary activity throughout the world, centuries of missionary activity confirms this. In her religious mission the church is intent on renewing every aspect of human life: social life, economics, politics and culture. Her message touches all fields of human endeavor. She blesses God for the progress of science and for everything that is being done in the world to help alleviate the condition of the sick, the needy, the poor. She herself is and will always remain in the forefront of efforts of service to the human person. And yet in all of this she reaffirms *the primacy of her spiritual vocation* and refuses to replace the proclamation of the kingdom of God by mere human activity.

The evangelizing church strives to encourage large numbers of Christians to devote themselves to the liberation of mankind. The church endeavors to provide the inspiration of faith and the motivation of Christian love to those who in turn will be Christian liberators. The church glories in her social teaching, which she constantly reaffirms and reasserts. We cannot assert too frequently the role of witness and the role of holiness in the work of evangelization.

Religious and the Call to Evangelize

The call to witness touches Religious in a very intimate way. Pope Paul VI has stated: "Religious for their part find in their consecrated life a privileged means of effective evangelization. At the deepest level of their being they are caught up in the dynamism of the Church's life, which is thirsty for the divine absolute and called to holiness. It is to this holiness that they bear witness. They embody the Church in their desire to give herself completely to the radical demands of the beatitudes. By their lives they are a sign of total availability to God, the Church and the brethren.

"As such, Religious have a special importance in the context of the witness which, as we have said, is of prime importance in evangelization. At the same time as being a challenge to the world and to the Church herself, this silent witness of poverty and abnegation, of purity and sincerity, of self-sacrifice and obedience, can become an eloquent witness capable of touching also non-Christians who have good will and are sensitive to certain values."

Still speaking about Religious the pope went on to give these insights: "Thanks to their consecration they are eminently willing and free to leave everything and to go and proclaim the gospel event to the ends of the earth. They are enterprising and their apostolate is often marked by originality, by a genius that demands admiration. They are generous: often they are found at the outposts of the mission and they take the greatest of risks for their health and their very lives. Truly the Church owes them much" (*Evangelii Nuntiandi*, 69).

This ideal is very high. It is very costly. It is very rewarding. How insightful of the pope *to link religious consecration with being enterprising in evangelization*, being marked by an originality and by a genius that demands admiration—and all of this linked with generosity, indeed with surrender!

Evangelization as a Work of the Church

In speaking about the identity of evangelization, we must also speak about *the identity of the evangelizer*. Once again the church wants us to realize that *evangelization is deeply ecclesial*. It is not an isolated act of an individual. It is part of the work of the church and this enhances the dignity of *every* evangelizer; it underlines in a special way the ecclesial dignity of the priests and Religious who evangelize. Whoever he or she may be, no evangelizer is the absolute master of the evangelizing action with the discretionary power to carry it out in accordance with individualistic criteria and perspectives. The evangelizer acts in communion with the church and with her pastors. This principle helps us to realize how much evangelization and the evangelizer belong to the church.

Evangelization disappears altogether if the evangelizer empties or adulterates *its content* under the pretext of adaptation or inculturation or for any other reason. We are called to collaborate, to lend our contribution to the great work of translating the treasure of faith, of helping to incarnate it in the lives of others within a vast legitimate variety of expressions. Yet we know that as ecclesial workers for evangelization we must do our part to preserve unaltered the content of the Catholic faith that the Lord entrusted to the apostles. For the rest there is open an area for vast ingenuity, originality and justifiable personal contributions to evangelization, which will always involve communicating Jesus Christ.

20. The Woman

Mother of God—Mother of the Redeemer

In his Letter to the Galatians St. Paul says: "When the fullness of time had come, God sent his Son, born of a woman, born under the law, to ransom those under the law, so that we might receive adoption" (Gal 4:4–5).

When Jesus dies on the cross he will address Mary by her title "woman." Invoking her as "woman," he will ratify her maternity over his church. For all generations she will be the Mother of his disciples; she will be the Mother of his body, the church. In the Apocalypse, the Book of Revelation, once again we shall find the title "woman." And the church will have recourse to this text in order *to honor Mary*, the Mother of Jesus and in order *to honor the church whose maternity she shares* and of whom *the woman Mary is the type and exemplar*.

The Second Vatican Council tells us that this woman Mary is indeed the Mother of God and the Mother of the Redeemer. It tells us that she herself was redeemed in an especially sublime manner by Christ, her Son, and that she is united to him by a close and unbreakable tie. This woman is endowed with the supreme office and dignity of being the Mother of the Son of God. As such, she is the favored daughter of the Father and the temple of the

Holy Spirit. She surpasses all creatures in heaven and on earth.

This woman, Mary, is honored by the Catholic Church as *the beloved Mother of us all* (cf. *Lumen Gentium*, 53). This woman Mary is a generous and faithful virgin. Her fruitful maternal love brought forth the Incarnate Word of God through a spousal relationship with the Holy Spirit, who overshadowed her. In bringing forth the Word of God, she likewise gave birth to the church, to all those who would be configured to her firstborn Son.

Type of the Church

The title "woman" is especially appropriate to Mary as she fulfills her role as the type and exemplar of the church, which is the bride of Christ. Mary, as the first of the redeemed, is the first member of the church but she also personifies the holiness of the entire church. Mary has already attained what all her sons and daughters will achieve in the course of centuries: sanctity in the church.

The woman Mary has an extraordinary role to play *in typifying the spousal relationship of the new creation.* The woman Mary is not only the Mother of the church and a member of the church; she embodies all of the holiness and fidelity of the church that is the result of God's new creation.

Here, it is important to realize that the two aspects of the spousal relationship of the new creation are exactly the same as those of the first creation: male and female. The masculinity and femininity of the first creation were designed to explain the second creation. *Christ is* presented to us in the scriptures as *the bridegroom of the church. The church is the bride.* This intimacy must always be maintained and extolled. This is why the church, in rightly maintaining a male priesthood to represent Jesus, will at the same time maintain as the supreme symbol of the spousal adherence of the church to Jesus generous, self-sacrificing, faithful, fruitful, virginal, maternal feminine love.

The Holy Father has asked the bishops to emphasize the special feminine role of women Religious. His words are: "In the Church and personifying the Church as the Spouse of Christ, they are called to live for Christ, faithfully, exclusively and permanently in the consciousness of being able to make visible the spousal aspect of the Church's love for Christ" (*Ad Limina* address to United States bishops, September 19, 1983). To emphasize how Religious are called to make visible the spousal aspect of the church's love for Christ is to emphasize how much they belong to the church, how much their vocation is part of the life that the church lives in union with Mary now glorified in her assumption.

The First of the Redeemed

In celebrating the assumption of Mary, we see her in all her glory, and we realize that the woman who is glorified is not only the Mother of God, the Mother of the Redeemer, the Mother of the church but she is also *the first of the redeemed.*

We wish to remember frequently that Christ died, in accordance with the Father's will, to save all mankind—all the descendants of Adam. Mary belonged to the race of Adam and therefore needed redemption. She received it. And the final sign of this redemption in her is the Assumption. But any treatment of the redemption of Mary brings us back to *the Immaculate Conception.* The Immaculate Conception was *God's gift to Mary in anticipation of the death of Jesus,* but also dependent on this death. When Jesus died, he thought of all of us, but he was dying above all for his Mother so that he might present her to his Father without spot or stain. He was dying to redeem his Mother so that she might in turn be a sign of sure hope for all of us, an intercessor for our holiness, that she might become "our life, our sweetness and our hope."

It was the foreseen merits of Christ's death that made Mary victorious in her Immaculate Conception, and the fullness of that victory is revealed in her assumption into heaven.

Extolling the Mystery of the Incarnation

By honoring Mary *we therefore imitate Jesus*; we do what he did. But we also proclaim and extol the divine mystery of the Incarnate Word. We proclaim that by the will of the Father, Jesus, his Eternal Son, becomes the Son of Mary. We acknowledge that the humanity of Jesus comes from Mary and that Jesus is Savior because of his sacred humanity.

All knowledge of God, of the Blessed Trinity, of the love and mercy of the Father comes to us *through the humanity of Jesus*. It is in his humanity that Jesus reveals the mercy and loving kindness of God. But it is Mary who supplied the humanity, and it is Mary who loved and brought up the child who was called upon to reveal love to the world.

When Jesus was dying on the cross, the thought of Mary's love and holiness gave him strength to suffer, strength to die on Calvary. *Devotion to Mary gives us strength to suffer*, strength to die, strength to live the life of Jesus.

Devotion to Mary links us to the essence of the mystery of Christianity: the incarnation. It acknowledges Mary's role of intercession on our behalf. It acknowledges her maternity in regard to all the church.

A Special Relationship to Mary

On our part our devotion to Mary is an act of faith, an act of hope, an act of love. In prayer we ask Mary to form Jesus in us, to bring his life, his holiness to perfection in us and in our brothers and sisters. Devotion to her means listening to her, especially when she says: "Do whatever he tells you" (John 2:5). This voice of hers that we hear at the wedding feast in Cana echoes the voice of the Eternal Father who says: "This is my beloved Son. Listen to him" (Mark 9:7).

Through Mary's intercession we are helped to observe the commandments even when they are difficult. She assists us to persevere in real charity—the charity that is linked to sacrifice. She preserves us in chastity of thought, word and action.

In our lives some small practices are necessary to show devotion to Mary. The *rosary* is a magnificent devotion; it has the blessing of the church and all the popes. It combines praise of Mary, with reflection on the mysteries of Christ.

Another excellent devotion is *consecration of ourselves to Mary*. This consecration to Mary involves entering into a special personal relationship with her—an act of entrusting to her one's self, one's mission, one's family, one's friends to obtain her loving intercession. Above all, it involves the entrusting of one's self to her maternal love in order *to be hers*.

For the Religious of the church, Mary will obtain the special grace *to exercise that spousal love proper to the church*, which they too personify together with her, so that in the church they may adhere to Jesus and from him receive all the love necessary for the satisfaction, fulfillment and joy of their lives. Through her intercession they receive strength for the apostolate.

It is wonderful to reflect how during the centuries the Religious of the church have shown immense honor to the Mother of God. They have edified and sustained the faithful in their veneration of Mary.

When we pray to Mary, reflecting on her words: "All generations will call me blessed," we have the power to summarize in our prayer, united with that of the church, all of the love shown to Mary over the centuries by the people of God. We are able to invoke and *offer to her all of the love of the Catholic Church* over two millennia. We are able to express the entire faith of the church that has been brought to fruition and beautiful expression in the dogmas of the church; the last one of which concerning Mary was defined on November 1, 1950. We are able to offer to Mary all of the devotion of the saints, the love of the Religious throughout the centuries and the millions of acts of devotion of simple people throughout the world, the millions of prayers addressed to her from prisons and prison camps, from suffering people, from Catholic homes, from parish churches, from millions of hearts.

Above all, because of our close relationship with her Son Jesus, our configuration to him and our identification with him by grace, we are able *to offer Mary all of the love that Jesus has ever shown her*, all of the love that is his as the Son of the Eternal Father and the Son of Mary. And in this filial relationship with her, we are able to present to her intercession all the needs of the church and all the needs of the world. In her hands we are able, over and over again, to ratify the church's consecration to Christ her Son and our own offering of our lives to her. We pray to Mary for the poor, the oppressed, the sick, the dying and those in sin. She is the hope of the dying, the consoler of the afflicted, the help of Christians, the cause of our joy. Through her all of us receive the grace to say: *"Jesus, I trust in you!"*

Femininity, Human Dignity and Love

At this time I wish to draw attention to the extended tribute given to our Blessed Mother by Pope John Paul II on his first pastoral visit to the United States. He spoke these words in the National Shrine of the Immaculate Conception: "My first desire is to direct my thoughts, to turn my heart to the woman of salvation history.

"In the eternal design of God, this woman, Mary, was chosen to enter into the work of the Incarnation and Redemption. And this design of God was to be actuated through her free decision given in obedience to the divine will. Through her *yes*—a *yes* that pervades and is reflected in all history she consented to be the Virgin Mother of our saving God, the handmaid of the Lord and, at the same time, the Mother of all the faithful who in the course of centuries would become the brothers and sisters of her Son.

"Through her, the Sun of Justice was to rise in the world. Through her, the great healer of humanity, the reconciler of hearts and consciences—her Son, the God-Man Jesus Christ—was to transform the human condition and, by his death and resurrection uplift the entire human family.

"As a great sign that appeared in the heavens in the fullness of time, the woman dominates all history as the Virgin Mother of the Son, and as the Spouse of the Holy Spirit—as the handmaid of humanity. And the woman becomes also—by association with her Son—the sign of contradiction to the world and, at the same time, the sign of hope whom all generations shall call blessed: the woman who conceived spiritually before she conceived physically; the woman who accepted the word of God; the woman who was inserted intimately and irrevocably into the mystery of the Church, exercising a spiritual motherhood with regard to all people; the woman who is honored as Queen of Apostles, without herself being inserted into the hierarchical constitution of the Church. And yet this woman made all hierarchy possible, because she gave to the world the Shepherd and Bishop of our souls.

"This woman, this Mary of the Gospel, who is not mentioned as being at the Last Supper, comes back again at the foot of the cross, in order to consummate her contribution to salvation history. By her courageous act, she prefigures and anticipates the courage of all women throughout the ages who concur in bringing forth Christ in every generation. At Pentecost, the Virgin Mother once again comes forward to exercise her role in union with the Apostles, with and in and over the Church. Yet again she conceives of the Holy Spirit, to bring forth Jesus in the fullness of his Body, the Church—never to leave him, never to abandon him, but to continue to love and serve him through the ages.

"This is the woman of history and destiny, who inspires us today; the woman who speaks to us of femininity, human dignity and love, and who is the greatest expression of total consecration to Jesus Christ..." (October 7, 1979).

21. Fidelity and Generosity Nurtured Daily

Saint Maximilian Mary Kolbe

Saint Maximilian Mary Kolbe gives us many opportunities to reflect on God's plan for our lives. Let me share with you an experience I had in Rome some years ago.

I was in a little restaurant one day for lunch. It was a Saturday, if I recall correctly, the very day before the beatification of Maximilian Mary Kolbe. Father Flaviano came in with an elderly gentleman. Father Flaviano was the Superior of the Community of Confessors in St. Peter's Basilica, the Community of the Franciscan Conventual Friars. We knew each other in the Vatican. Father Flaviano also used to come to Los Angeles; he had celebrated Mass a number of times in my home parish, Cathedral Chapel.

In the course of the lunch he came over to my table and asked me to come over to his. He wanted to introduce me to his guest. The guest, who had come for the beatification, was special indeed, having an air of great simplicity and dignity. He was very much involved in the event of the beatification because he was *the man for whom St. Maximilian had given his life*. They had both been in the Auschwitz concentration camp together. The year was 1941. The Nazis had decided to kill a number of the prisoners; it did not matter who, provided they reached their quota.

Maximilian stepped forward to ask to take the place of a married man with children. Maximilian was completely available to God and to his neighbor. "I am a Catholic priest," he said, "and I am old; I want to take his place because he has a wife and children." He was really not old, but in God's providence he was old enough to die, even though he was only forty-seven. There was no problem for the Nazis. It really did not matter who died for the Nazi cause. Maximilian Mary Kolbe's request was granted without delay. He was then left to starve to death. Two weeks later he was given a lethal injection. It was August 14 and his time had come; he could celebrate the feast of the assumption in heaven with our Blessed Mother. For such a long time he had assiduously promoted devotion to Mary.

A few years later, the pope who beatified Maximilian Kolbe, Paul VI, had been succeeded by a Polish pope. In 1982 John Paul II canonized Maximilian as a martyr of the church. The clear message of the canonization was that: "No one has greater love than this, to lay down one's life for one's friends" (John 15:13).

Once again the man for whom St. Maximilian gave his life came back to Rome for the canonization. There was a huge ovation in St. Peter's Square as John Paul II embraced him before the world. Once again it was shown that: "God writes straight with crooked lines."

The prophet Ezekiel describes the story of infidelity on the part of God's people, of an oath that was rejected and a covenant that was broken. And yet, although the spouse of God is unfaithful, the prophet Ezekiel testifies that God will of course still pardon her and maintain with her an eternal covenant (cf. Ezek 16).

By contrast, the message of St. Maximilian Kolbe is *a message of fidelity, generosity, total surrender.* To understand his victory, one must understand his whole history of fidelity and generosity as a Religious, his missionary zeal in Japan, his service to others, his love for Mary. The supreme act of his love and his martyrdom did not just happen. God prepared him for years and he responded faithfully, day by day, year by year. In his final sacrifice at Auschwitz he expressed the sentiments that he had nurtured thousands of times before: *Jesus, I trust in you!*

In the gospel Jesus repeatedly talks about renunciation, including the renunciation of marriage for the kingdom of heaven. This renunciation was part of St. Maximilian Kolbe's offering of his life to God, part of the way whereby God prepared him for his acts of daily heroism and service.

Saint Maximilian is a great triumph of Christ's precious blood and a great triumph of Mary's intercession. His example is a great incentive to our fidelity and generosity.

22. Religious Consecration

The call of Jesus to his first apostles was something unique in the life of the church. And yet there are two elements in this call that are supremely important for all consecrated life and mission. We must emphasize these two elements repeatedly. Jesus called the apostles *to be with him* and *to be sent forth* (cf. Mark 3:14). *Intimacy with Christ is essential to consecration.* It precedes and accompanies all evangelizing activity.

Not only did Jesus call his apostles, but he prayed to his Father *to consecrate them in truth* (cf. John 17:17). After telling us this in the Gospel of St. John, Jesus also tells us that he consecrates himself for his apostles so that they may be consecrated in truth. Here we see that Jesus is the supreme consecrated one, the supreme missionary of the Father for the sake of his kingdom.

An attraction to consecrated life in the church is indeed an attraction to the supreme consecrated one and to his way of life—to the way Christ lives in the communion of his Father and the Holy Spirit, in the way that the apostles were companions of Jesus.

Inseparable to the Life and Holiness
of the Church

The Second Vatican Council gives us indeed
many insights into religious life. It is these insights
that in the postconciliar period have been developed,
and reflected upon under the inspiration of the Holy
Spirit and have been repeatedly proposed in the magisterium of the church, and in particular by the
teaching of the Holy Father. It is always good, however, to return to the Second Vatican Council to see
the clarity with which it taught and continues to
inspire the people of God. The Council speaks about
religious consecration and tells us that it "belongs
inseparably to the life and holiness of the Church"
(*Lumen Gentium*, 44).

And so, in speaking about consecration in the
church we are speaking about the life and holiness of
the church.

The simplicity of the insights of the people of God
is indeed correct. *Consecration means belonging to Christ*
and in him being related to the Most Blessed Trinity.
In *Vita Consecrata*, the important postsynodal apostolic exhortation on consecrated life, which is useful
for ongoing reflection and prayer, the Holy Father
writes as follows: "The consecrated life, deeply rooted
in the example and teaching of Christ the Lord, is a
gift of God the Father to his Church, through the
Holy Spirit. By the profession of the evangelical counsels, *the characteristic features of Jesus*—the chaste, poor
and obedient one—*are made constantly 'visible' in the*

midst of the world and in the eyes of the faithful are directed to the mystery of the kingdom of God, already at work in history, even as it awaits its full realization in heaven" (no. 1).

This element, which is consecration, is a lofty ideal in the church. It is a great treasure for which the popes have constantly thanked God and which they have repeatedly encouraged the church to maintain in authentic forms.

In June 1998, I was in Rome for the *Ad Limina* visit of Region IX of the U.S. bishops. During our visit with the Holy Father, he devoted his entire discourse to the ideal of religious consecration in the church. Among the many reflections that he made in this discourse there was the following: "Religious communities themselves need to reaffirm their confidence in their calling and, relying on the help of the Holy Spirit, repropose the ideal of consecration and mission. A presentation of the evangelical counsels merely in terms of their usefulness and convenience for a particular form of service is not enough. It is *only personal experience, through faith, of Christ and of the mystery of his kingdom at work in human history* which can make the ideal come alive in the minds and hearts of those who may be called" (Address of June 13, 1998, no. 5). The consecration of Religious starts with a personal experience of Christ and his church and it leads into the depth of the trinitarian life of God. From this trinitarian life, it leads forth to share the mission of Jesus in the world.

There are many consequences flowing from religious consecration, just as religious consecration is linked to baptism and reaffirms the commitments of baptism. These include: to be with Christ, to be his companions, to experience him in faith, to be called to enter into the intimacy of the life of the Most Blessed Trinity in a way particularly blessed by the church. The documents of the Holy See, especially *Vita Consecrata*, give us numerous possibilities for reflection on the great gift of religious consecration and on the demands that it makes on those who have generously accepted it as a gift of the Father through Jesus.

I would like to limit myself to a few reflections based on the teaching of the church as it has been highlighted and emphasized in this postconciliar period.

Prayer

It makes great sense to think of prayer as one of the first requirements of religious consecration in the church. It is easy to see, in selecting certain aspects of religious life for special reflection, that the notion of prayer stands out immediately. The Code of Canon Law states that *the first and principal duty of all Religious is the contemplation of things divine, and constant union with God in prayer* (cf. *Canon* 663, par. §1). We can see then that the question of Religious being united with God in prayer precedes the question of what activity they will perform. We know that prayer keeps alive our relationship with Christ. It is very basic to companionship with Jesus.

Permit me to go back to another source of inspiration and that is the exhortation that our Holy Father gave to the women Religious of the United States on the occasion of his first pastoral visit to our country in 1979. On that occasion he said the following: "Christ remains primary in your life only when he enjoys the first place in your mind and heart. Thus you must continuously unite yourself to him in prayer. Without prayer, religious life has no meaning. It has lost contact with its source, it has emptied itself of substance and it no longer can fulfill its goal. Without prayer there can be no joy, no hope, no peace. For prayer is what keeps us in touch with Christ" (October 7, 1979).

These incisive words of Pope John Paul II and those of Pope Paul VI written in *Evangelica Testificatio* call us all to reflect: "Do not forget the witness of history. Faithfulness to prayer or its abandonment is the test of the vitality or decadence of religious life" (*Evangelica Testificatio*, 42).

In 1983, Pope John Paul II, during the *Ad Limina* visit of the bishops of the United States at that time, also devoted an entire discourse to religious life. He asked the bishops on that occasion to thank the Religious of the United States for the immense contribution that they have made to the church in our country. He was very intent to say that their greatest dignity consists in this: "That Religious are persons individually called by God and consecrated by God through the mediation of his Church. The value of their activity is great, but the value of who they are is greater still" (September 19, 1983). Religious are who they are precisely because the church mediates their consecration and guarantees their charism to be Religious. We can see then that consecration is so much a part of the identity of consecrated persons, so much a part of their dignity.

Ecclesial Identity

An element that needs constantly to be emphasized because it is a source of immense inspiration for Religious themselves is the fact that *it is absolutely essential that all Religious live in union with the church.* Religious are who they are because the church makes them who they are.

Pursuing this ecclesial identity of Religious, the Holy Father then went on to situate it in the full and complete acceptance of the church's magisterium. Permit me to give another quote from this same *Ad Limina* discourse: "And may everyone realize that *the greatest misunderstanding* of the charism of Religious, indeed the greatest offense to their dignity and their persons would come from those who might try *to situate their life or mission outside its ecclesial context.* Religious are betrayed by anyone who would attempt to have them embrace teaching against the magisterium of the Church, who conceived them by her love and gave them birth in her liberating truth. The acceptance of the reality of the Church by Religious and their vital union—through her and in her—with Christ is *an essential condition for the vitality of their prayer*, the effectiveness of their service to the poor, the validity of their social witness, the well-being of their community relationships, the measure of the success of their renewal and the guarantee of the authenticity of their poverty and simplicity of life. And only in total union with the Church does their chastity become the full and acceptable gift which will satisfy the craving of their hearts to give themselves to Christ and to receive from him, and to be faithful in his love."

All consecrated persons can understand the tremendous esteem and love that the church has for them. All the bishops are witnesses of this esteem and love. To these persons the church says: it is because of your consecration, it is because of your calling to be with Jesus and to be his companions. *Consecration is God's free gift to you, through the church.* It is God who consecrates you. It is the church that mediates this consecration and it is your gift of freedom that lovingly accepts the gift of the Most Blessed Trinity. For all of this the people of God love you and pray for you, and Jesus continues to pray for you that you may be always consecrated in truth. You are consecrated in a specific religious family. There is something very personal in your consecration. Each one of you has joined a congregation that has been established and recognized and sustained by the church. All of this is meant to be, in order *that all of you may be with Christ and then be sent out on mission.*

As consecrated persons you are called *to serve in a particular way the holiness of God's people*. You are called like Mary to be a sign of the holiness of Christ's church. You are called to be worthy of the consecration that Christ and his church offer to you, the privilege of belonging entirely to God.

"We Cannot Live Without Love."

Your life is indeed a life that makes no sense without prayer. Your life makes no sense without love, and we know that without prayer there cannot be sustained love. Once again let us listen to our Holy Father Pope John Paul II: "Two dynamic forces are operative in religious life: your love for Jesus—and, in Jesus, for all who belong to him—and his love for you.

"We cannot live without love. If we do not encounter love, if we do not experience it and make it our own, and if we do not participate intimately in it our life is meaningless. Without love we remain incomprehensible to ourselves (cf. *Redemptor Hominis*, 10).

"Thus every one of you needs a vibrant relationship of love to the Lord, a profound loving union with Christ, your spouse. A love like that expressed in the Psalm: 'God, you are my God whom I seek, for you my flesh pines and my soul thirsts like the earth, parched, lifeless and without water. Thus have I gazed toward you in the sanctuary to see your power and your glory' (Ps 63:1–2).

"Yet far more important than your love for Christ is Christ's love for you. You have been called by him, made a member of his body, consecrated in a life of the evangelical counsels and destined by him to have a share in the mission that Christ has entrusted to the Church: his own mission of salvation. For this reason, you center your life in the Eucharist. In the Eucharist, you celebrate his death and resurrection and receive from him the bread of eternal life. And it is in the Eucharist especially that you are united to the one who is the object of all your love. Here with him, you find ever-greater reason to love and serve his brothers and sisters. Here, with him—with Christ —you find greater understanding and compassion for God's people and here you find the strength to persevere in your commitment to selfless service" (address to women Religious, October 7, 1979).

For all consecrated persons these words of Pope John Paul II are very special: "Yet far more important than your love for Christ is Christ's love for you." This explains so much of religious consecration. It explains Religious to themselves and it more than requires their response of trust: *Jesus, I trust in you!*

23. Mission of Catechetics or Catechesis

Answering the Plea of the World: "We Want to See Jesus."

Consecrated Religious whose mission is catechetics or catechesis deserve great support. This mission is so much a part of their consecrated life. I have already spoken about the general mission of the church, *evangelization*, in which the church finds her "deepest identity."

We know that evangelization has many aspects, many "moments" to it. Catechetics or catechesis is one of these "moments" and we know that for many religious families this is *a corporate apostolate*.

Taking into account the need for a certain degree of flexibility, Pope John Paul II has emphasized during the last *Ad Limina* visit of the U.S. bishops of Region IX the importance of a corporate apostolate. His words to that group of bishops, of whom I was one, were these: "... an institute's capacity to conduct a common or community apostolate is of vital concern to the life of a particular Church. It is not enough that all members of an institute subscribe to the same general values or work 'according to the founding spirit' with each one responsible for finding some place of apostolic activity and a residence. Obviously, not every member of an institute will be suited to work in only one apostolate, but the identity and nature of the common apostolate, and the willingness to engage in it, should be an essential part of an institute's discerning of the vocation of its candidates" (June 15, 1998).

You may know more than I do about how catechesis works in a very practical way. But I would like to reflect with you today on what a stupendous reality catechesis is in the life of the church. This is not meant to be a theological treatise, but rather a reflection on catechesis as *a vital component of the mission of Religious*—that mission which is so linked to religious consecration. This may well be a moment for Religious to reflect on their mission and on the reason you pursue it, to reflect on the dignity of their corporate work and the value that it has for the church.

My comments are meant to reflect the content of the apostolic exhortation *Catechesi Tradendae*. This document was the fruit of the work of three popes and one synod. The synod was held in the pontificate of Pope Paul VI. The document was begun before his death. It was continued by his successor Pope John Paul I, and transmitted for completion to his successor, Pope John Paul II. It was then issued on October 16, 1979, the first anniversary of the election of Pope John Paul II.

The document should be a font of joy for Religious who catechize because it draws attention to what you do and who you are as catechists in the life of the church. The beginning of the document speaks about the joy of bringing the mystery of Christ to the world. This is what you are involved in. This is the life that you are leading and the mission that is yours.

Communicating Christ

The pope speaks about the primary and essential object of catechesis as being the mystery of Christ. He says: "The definitive aim of catechesis is to put people not only in touch but in communion, in intimacy, with Jesus Christ" (*Catechesi Tradendae*, 5). It is obvious that all catechizing activity is Christocentric. In catechesis it is Christ the Incarnate Word and Son of God who is taught. Everything else is taught in reference to him. In speaking about this element of teaching, the Holy Father emphasizes not only that it is Christ who is taught, but also that it is Christ alone who teaches and everyone else who teaches does so only to the extent that he or she teaches in the name of Christ. Here too we have a wonderful understanding of the role of catechesis in the church. Here we begin to understand that, as we teach Christ and as we enter into the role of Christ as he teaches himself, our own role is to imitate Jesus who said: "My teaching is not my own but is from the one who sent me" (John 7:16).

All of this tells us that catechesis is not the teaching of abstract truths. It is the communication of the living Christ, and it is possible only if the teacher has been with Christ, only if the teacher is his companion, only if there is intimacy with the master.

What a privilege it is for you to be engaged in an activity to which the church has given such great priority. The Holy Father has insisted on this priority saying: "The Church is bidden by God and by events —each of them a call from him—to renew her trust in catechetical activity as a prime aspect of her mission" (*Catechesi Tradendae*, 15).

To approach the apostolic task of teaching "with a fresh outlook" is also reflected in the Holy Father's apostolic exhortation. He speaks about the need to be continually renewed by the revision of catechetical methods, by the search for suitable language and by the utilization of new means of transmitting the message that is Jesus. You are called to contribute to the proper inculturation of the gospel. No small task!

Organic and Systematic Teaching

In everything the church does she looks upon catechesis as a stage of evangelization, a special moment. Between catechesis and evangelization there is no separation; neither are the two simply identical. The Holy Father tells us that catechesis is an education in the faith which, generally speaking, imparts the teaching of Christian doctrine in an organic and systematic way with a view to initiating the hearers into the fullness of Christian life. "The specific character of catechesis," he says, "...has the twofold objective of maturing the initial faith and of educating the true disciple of Christ by means of a deeper and more systematic knowledge of the person and the message of our Lord Jesus Christ" (*Catechesi Tradendae*, 19).

We can see that within the whole process of evangelization the aim of catechesis is to be *the teaching and the maturation stage* in which the human person endeavors to know Jesus Christ ever more deeply.

For all those like yourselves engaged in this apostolate there is a need to offer a systematic teaching. The Holy Father spells out this challenge for the church. Catechesis must not be improvised. It must deal with essentials. It must be sufficiently complete and not stop at the initial proclamation of the Christian mystery such as we have in *the kerygma*. It must be an integral Christian initiation. It seems to me that this challenge of the Holy Father becomes for you an exhilarating opportunity to reflect on your own mission of collaboration in the church of Christ. Since catechesis is a particular moment in evangelization, the content of the two are indeed the same. The good news of salvation means *the explicit proclamation and communication of Jesus*: the name of Jesus, his teaching, his life, his promises, his kingdom, his commandments, his church, his full identity as Son of God and Son of Mary, as Redeemer of the world.

As you might expect, the Holy Father has emphasized, in a work as important as catechesis, the need for *the integrity of the content*, and for *suitable pedagogical methods*. In working toward these aims, what magnificent creativity, originality—including the originality of prayer and meditation—can be offered to the church by those like yourselves who collaborate in her mission of catechesis. A particularly challenging element in catechesis is the ecumenical dimension. The Holy Father is not shy in approaching this dimension and in recommending its inclusion, but at the same time he reminds us that the fullness of the revealed truths and of the means of salvation instituted by Christ is found in the Catholic Church. In this he faithfully draws on the Second Vatican Council (*Unitatis Redintegratio*, 3).

Importance of Catechetics

As a bishop I obviously have a special interest in this topic because, as the pope says: "If catechesis is done well in your local Churches, everything else will be easier to do" (*Catechesi Tradendae*, 63). Once again we see not only the priority set by the Holy Father but also, behind the priority, his passion to communicate the mystery of Christ as something that has a profound impact on every local church and on the universal church.

The Holy Father not only wants to encourage you in the work of catechesis, but he is asking for your full collaboration. He needs you. He expresses it in these words: "I wholeheartedly exhort you whose religious consecration should make you even more readily available for the Church's service, to prepare as well as possible for the task of catechesis according to the differing vocations of your institutes and the missions entrusted to you, and to carry this concern everywhere. Let the communities dedicate as much as possible of what ability and means they have to the specific work of catechesis" (*ibid.*, 65).

Wherever you are, there is the opportunity to communicate Christ, and to do this in an organic and systematic way. You do it through the power of your witness, through the consistency of your testimony and through the joy of your activity.

I have already mentioned that Christ is the teacher in catechesis, that he is the one who catechizes. And yet we know that the Holy Spirit completes the teaching of Christ. Jesus himself says that the Spirit will bear witness to him and that we also are his witnesses because the Spirit transforms us into witnesses of Christ (cf. John 15:26–27).

I offer for your reflection then these various considerations in order to highlight and emphasize *the dignity* that has been given to you *in your ecclesial role as catechists*. What is involved in your mission is putting people into contact with the person of Jesus, transmitting Christ's teaching according to his command, being an instrument of Christ the teacher, being conformed to the person of Christ by the Holy Spirit who completes the work of Christ. Is there more that adds to the dignity of your mission? Yes, it is *the connection that exists between what you say and what you do and who you are*. Every sector of your being works together in the mission of communicating Jesus to others, and the intensity of your life of grace is a special requirement for you to be effective in the catechetical apostolate. Your union lived and cultivated with Christ and through Christ with the

Most Blessed Trinity is an effective gauge of your fruitfulness in catechetics.

Remember, Jesus says: "I am the vine, you are the branches" (John 15:5). If we are cut off from him, obviously there is no salutary activity on our part, since the degree of our union with him is also the degree of our effectiveness in performing a work that is so clearly and completely his. You are called to teach by your life just as Christ did. The Holy Father asks you to remember: "That the majesty of Christ the Teacher and the unique consistency and persuasiveness of his teaching can only be explained by the fact that his words, his parables and his arguments are never separable from his life and his very being" (*Catechesi Tradendae*, 9).

How much the Holy Father counts on Religious in the mission of catechesis! I cannot emphasize enough his words: "Let the communities dedicate as much as possible of what ability and means they have to the specific work of catechesis" (*ibid.*, 65). To accept the pope's invitation is to express the love and obedience that bind you in consecrated life to the successor of Peter and to his ministry of service in the church.

"We Want to See Jesus."

You can see how many people need your help. You can see the extraordinary value that the church attaches to your mission. You can see the relationship between your consecration to Jesus and the mission that the church has entrusted to you. You can see that the challenge is enormous but that Jesus will always be there to respond to your prayer: *Jesus, I trust in you!*

You can see that the world is truly speaking to you in those words recorded in St. John's Gospel that the Greeks addressed to Philip: "We would like to see Jesus" (John 12:21).

And as you face this challenge, this exhilarating ecclesial work, know that our Blessed Mother is there to help you. Mary is indeed "a living catechism"; she is indeed the Mother and model of all catechists. She has *experience in communicating Jesus to the world.*

24. Consecrated Chastity Lived In Joy

The Second Vatican Council speaks to us about the evangelical counsels, calling them divine gifts "which the Church has received from her Lord and which she ever preserves with the help of his grace" (*Lumen Gentium*, 43).

We are considering the evangelical counsels in the context of the gift of consecration to God. The evangelical counsels are the means by which the great gift of consecration is lived. The evangelical counsel of chastity is an essential part of God's overall gift of religious consecration.

The risen Lord Jesus alone can inspire consecrated chastity and sustain it. The chastity of which we are speaking is intimately linked to the surrender of our freedom to God in love. Consecrated chastity is truly a powerful means to belong to God, to accept the love of Christ as all-fulfilling, all-satisfying and all-encompassing.

At the core of our being is the mystery of human sexuality with its powers of communication, self-giving and receiving from another, together with its sensual craving for satisfaction.

Renunciation and Gift

The chastity of the evangelical counsel is the gift of all of this to the Lord, the surrender for the sake of the kingdom of heaven, for the love of Jesus, for the redemption of the world. Here there are two elements: *renunciation* and *gift*. They are closely linked. Renunciation is already a gift, when motivated by love, but it must always be offered explicitly as a gift to God.

Realism tells us that this gift of consecrated chastity must be made under the sign of *self-denial and sustained discipline*. There is nothing that we can say or do that will make this abnegation easy, or take away from our hearts the desire to be loved, or remove from our bodies the concupiscence of the flesh. We must continually recall the immense value of the gift. We must also recall its significance for the church and her apostolate and the means at our disposal for its preservation.

What then is the value of the gift? It is in *the offering of the person* at the core of his or her being, in the sphere of freedom, with sacrifice and love. The church has to guarantee us this value, and she does. True spousal love shows us the qualities that chaste consecrated love must have. It is faithful, perpetual and exclusive. Christ's spousal love for his church shows these qualities.

This type of love helps make the church what she is meant to be, a total clinging or adherence to the Lord in anticipation of the Parousia. In other words, it is *an expression of the holiness of the church*, and this holiness is a supernatural means for proclaiming Christ.

Need for God's Help

The means for the preservation of consecrated chastity certainly include *prayer*. We need an understanding of ourselves in the light of Christ, who we are called to be by grace, and the strength we need. In prayer we must make an explicit, sustained and persevering call for help. We also need *penance*. It must accompany a realization of our weakness and be expressed in some form of mortification. We cannot do everything we want; we cannot indulge completely even all our licit desires and expect to have strength in the face of concupiscence. We need *vigilance*, which takes into account the total lifestyle of the celibate Religious. In the lifestyle of consecrated chastity everything is different from that of Christian married love or even the chaste love of a single person. Satisfaction, fulfillment, fruitfulness and joy are on a different level. Vigilance must be accompanied by discipline, patience, perseverance and peace. It must exclude anxiety.

Realism compels us to reflect on *temptations* and *occasions of sin*. It compels us to consider the thoughts, words, actions and omissions that can lead to *deep compromise*, to *acts of rationalization* and then to *the state of having a dulled conscience*. At this point, rationalization can become a real danger in our lives. It can prompt us to embrace new theories in order to circumvent chastity. Satan can disguise himself as an angel of light. Under the guise of a new ecclesiology, or a loving relationship, or the exigencies of our humanity, we can completely alienate ourselves from our commitment and claim justification in other forms of so-called loving service and prophetic leadership—which no longer demand the renunciation of the flesh.

In another context, St. Paul spoke of those who are "false apostles, deceitful workers, who masquerade as apostles of Christ" (2 Cor 11:13).

The long history of the spiritual life in the church and the witness of the magisterium testify to the value of *frequent confession* as a help for living chastity in all its renunciation, but also in its fulfilling and exhilarating aspect of "offer[ing] our bodies," in the expression of St. Paul, "as a living sacrifice, holy and pleasing to God" (Rom 12:1). And this living and holy sacrifice St. Paul calls "spiritual worship."

Frequent confession in itself contains an immense source of grace, which is the passion of Christ. It is also a faith-filled expression both of *the acknowledgment of human weakness and of the need for God's help.* It is a means of grace and strength that confirms us in vigilance and needed perseverance.

The effects of celibate love are indeed beautiful. Through chastity, Religious are able to love with the love of Christ and to experience his love for themselves. Certainly the living of celibacy in the modern world is still difficult. Its struggle is part of the struggle for the kingdom of God. It is part of *the witness to the primacy of God* and to *the holiness of Christ in his church*. At different times in our lives, the struggle can be most intense, the effort more demanding. But *the effort* and *the struggle* themselves are *a hymn of praise*, of confidence and hope to the Lord, who is able to bring about in us far more than we could ask or imagine (cf. Eph 3:20).

Hope in the Living God

For this we labor and struggle as we do, for we have placed our hope in the living God. This hope is supremely expressed in the Eucharist, where our oblation of celibacy through the action of the Holy Spirit is fused with the sacrifice of Jesus in one great act of love for the Father and for the salvation of the world. A consciousness of this continues to call us to renunciation, constant conversion and greater surrender in love.

There are millions of people hidden in the church, including young people, who are practicing chastity, according to their state in life, despite difficulties and the great obstacles posed by the sexual revolution. Each one of these participates in the victory of the risen Lord. Obstacles besiege you too, but they are never sufficient in themselves to obstruct the paschal victory of the Lord Jesus.

We must pray that through chastity, lived in celibacy, we may bear witness to the power of the risen Jesus to attract us to himself and to possess us totally: body and soul, mind, heart and will.

It is no surprise how celibacy and even chastity itself is despised in some quarters. And what is said of chastity can apply to so many other ideals of the religious life—and the Christian life also. You have to brace yourselves for opposition to everything as a matter of fact—to all your ideals, even from some within the church and within religious life. And so you know that the fidelity that you exercise in faithfully observing consecrated chastity will be mocked and ridiculed by some. You will be accused of being "out of it," of being naive, or whatever.

Remember, rather, the church assures you of the tremendous value of your observance of this evangelical counsel. The church assures you of *the profound meaning of your life of consecrated chastity* lived in joy. The church assures you of the grace of God.

By means of the renunciation and the gift, by means of the surrender of yourselves to Christ, you are opened *to be filled with his transforming love*. More than this no one can ask.

As we can see, it is extremely necessary to hope in God, to trust in Jesus. The hope that Religious have to remain in consecrated chastity is a hope that is linked to the virtue of *humility*, whereby they recognize their weaknesses and their limitations. But this hope is also linked to the virtue of *magnanimity* whereby they are willing to dare to be generous in undertaking an arduous enterprise. Convinced that the Christ who has called them will sustain them to the end, they pray: *Jesus, I trust in you!*

25. Evangelical Poverty: Gift and Challenge to Consecrated Religious

Does it surprise you to hear that evangelical poverty is one of the greatest challenges of religious consecrated life today in the church? Obviously not. You are striving to live this challenge in the spirit of your consecration with love and trust, saying: *Jesus, I trust in you!* To face this challenge there is only one adequate means: *to look to Jesus.* We must understand the role of poverty in religious life only by turning to Jesus. To see what he said about poverty, how he treated it, how he presented it, how he recommended it, but above all how he lived it—*what poverty meant for the Incarnate Word.*

We can see right away that the only reason the church talks about poverty is because of Jesus and his word. The world would certainly never tell you to be poor; the world would never help you to discover value in this evangelical counsel.

I will have nothing new to tell you about poverty, but I know that being in religious life *you have the gift.* Obviously you must explore its meaning constantly, but you also have the grace to understand the gift and to live it humbly, lovingly and effectively— in response to Christ, who gave you your vocation to religious life, to chastity, poverty and obedience.

Two important principles must be established. The first is that Jesus Christ is the reward for poverty, and second that renunciation along with free surrender is a response to Christ.

Sharing God's Gifts

The idea of sharing God's gifts with others, of keeping nothing for yourselves, of striving to provide love for the poor in their different types of needs is marvelously integrated into the gift of poverty. You are called to share in the way that the church asks you to share. You are called to share what you have in your life of poverty with those whom God places in your path. God's constant care that utilizes your provident love for the poor has its exigencies. You cannot walk over the poor in front of you, thinking that God is calling you to make a more judicious selection somewhere down the road.

Let me share with you an example that may be useful to you in your evaluation of service to the poor. Some years ago I was speaking to a Religious who was engaged in Catholic education in a large school in the capital of another country. The school was in one of the poorest sections of the city. The Religious explained to me her desire to do something more for the poor. She wanted to reach out in personal service—a different kind of service—to alleviate the needs of the poor. I asked her: "And if you go away, will there be someone to replace you, will there be someone to replace you that loves the poor as

much as you do?" And the answer was: "I am sure."
But I asked: "Are you really sure?" Then I ventured
to offer another suggestion. "Don't you think that the
work you are doing is a tremendous service to the
poor? Uplifting them in their human need for education, bringing them a deeper knowledge of God,
offering them the means to greater human and Christian advancement?" And the answer was: "I didn't
look at it that way." I thanked the Sister for her love
and zeal for the poor. I asked her to think once more
about her decision. She said she would.

For generations the church has been with the poor
in so many different ways. It all goes back to Jesus,
who was conscious of the prophecy of Isaiah as
applied to himself: "The spirit of the Lord GOD is
upon me . . . / He has sent me to bring glad tidings to
the lowly" (Isa 61:1–2; cf. Luke 4:16).

Following Jesus

We know that *evangelical poverty is a response to a
gift of God.* In the nineteenth chapter of St. Matthew's
Gospel we have a powerful recommendation from
Jesus to the rich young man. It is interesting and
important to note the various elements of Jesus' discourse. They can basically be summed up in his words:
"If you would be perfect, go, sell what you have and
give to the poor and come, follow me." The bottom
line is: come, follow me! But the conditions are: go,
sell, give to the poor. As we know, giving to the poor

manifests itself in so many different types of service. The reaction of the young man causes us to reflect. The gospel tells us that he had many possessions and he wanted to keep them. Therefore he went away sad. He took the exit of escape, escape from the invitation of Jesus.

But what Jesus is proposing is the opposite of escape. He is offering special joy to Religious in the following of himself. But once again, as in chastity, there are two elements that make up evangelical poverty: *renunciation* and *gift*. The power to cling to Christ requires previous renunciation. The condition is laid down by Jesus himself: "If you want to be perfect...!" But why poverty? Why renunciation? Here we are back in mystery—the mystery of holiness, where we can single out two elements, humanly speaking, of human holiness: separation from what is not God and adherence to God, in Christ. The reasoning behind this is the same general principle as in celibate chastity: to divest ourselves in order to follow Jesus, to possess him, and in him to contemplate and possess the Father and the Holy Spirit.

In other words, it is *a question of renunciation in order to possess*. Psalm 16:5 says: "LORD, my allotted portion and my cup." By profession, the Religious is called to proclaim to the world that all its riches are not enough; they do not fulfill, they do not satisfy the human heart. But we know that renunciation is fulfilling, not of itself but because of what it permits the person to seize: namely Jesus Christ and his

171

riches. Remember the expression of St. Paul: "so that you are not lacking in any spiritual gift" (1 Cor 1:7).

To see how this works, we may profitably look to the saints. But let us now turn directly to Jesus, asking: *What did he accomplish by poverty?* Here St. Paul has something to tell us: "For you know the gracious act of our Lord Jesus Christ, that for your sake he became poor although he was rich, so that by his poverty you might become rich" (2 Cor 8:9). What value did poverty have in the life of Jesus? *It enriched his church!*

Dependence on the Father

But there is another aspect of poverty in the life of Jesus. It is so sublime that it is hard to fathom and express. Let us ask the Holy Spirit to let us grasp this reality: not only what Christ accomplished by poverty but what it meant for him in his sacred humanity and even in his divine personhood. *Poverty brings with it a dependence on another.* In poverty one depends on God.

Consecrated poverty means possessing nothing of one's own. At this point the world will mightily contest the relevance of such a charism and virtue. In religious life there are those who would not be in agreement with this either. But in this very sense, poverty was verified in the human nature of Jesus and even in his divine person!

Jesus constantly tried to explain that *he possesses nothing of his own, he depends totally on his Father.* This is true. Jesus holds all from the Father. He is the image of the Father, the Father's word. He is the splendor of the Father. In terms of theology, he exists as the second person of the Most Blessed Trinity totally in relation to the Father. His person is generated by the Father and his existence is totally directed to the Father. This is what is meant in the beautiful theological formula: *Totus ad Patrem*. His human nature depends on the divinity. It possesses no human personality. Jesus is not a human person; he is a divine person. Jesus depends   and he loves to repeat it—totally on the Father. Jesus expresses this mystery in many ways in the Gospel of St. John. He says: "My teaching is not my own but is from the one who sent me" (John 7:16). And again: "I can do nothing of my own, but I only say what the Father taught me" (John 8:28). And again, Jesus exclaims: "[Father] everything of mine is yours and everything of yours is mine" (John 17:10). Jesus is the Son of the Father's love (cf. Col 1:13). He has absolutely nothing of his own. His Sonship exists only in relation to the Father. He is "God from God, Light from Light, true God from true God."

Is all this really relevant? Yes, this dependence on the Father—one of the deepest and most notable characteristics of the existence of Jesus—is the model for religious poverty as a means of following the Jesus who said: "*Go, sell, give, and come follow me.*" There are many aspects to be pondered in the gift of poverty, but here we are at its heart.

Need for Wisdom

For Religious, excessive possessions and a spirit of attachment are incompatible with possessing Jesus Christ. Lay people's rightful use and possession of goods are dictated by their vocation. Religious have a different mission—a special configuration to the Jesus who possesses nothing but who yet vindicates to himself all that the Father possesses.

Here Religious must be guided by their constitutions in *a constant revision of their lifestyle* under the inspiration of the Holy Spirit and at the direction of the church. But here too Religious must be challenged to meditate not only on the way they live but on who they are, what they possess and what they should really possess. Certainly poverty can never mean having everything you want, when you want it, the way you want it.

This strong challenge is a challenge that is common to institutions in the church, to many religious families. It is not enough to decide once and for all to live simply. Poverty, like chastity, requires constant vigilance. *The Holy Spirit continually has something to say to Religious about poverty.* They are faced with the need to discern the signs of the times, but one thing is certain: "The Son of Man has nowhere to rest his head" (Matt 8:20).

In the whole question of possessions there is need for balanced discernment and great prudence, but this is not enough. What is especially needed is wisdom! Whatever God has given to the community must be used well. It must be preserved with diligence and, when material goods are in fact lacking, you must be patient.

You know that, like Jesus, you must depend totally on the Father. You must continually renounce possessions in order to possess Jesus and to share him with others. And when you do possess him and share him, you will be able to say: "The LORD is my shepherd; / there is nothing I lack" (Ps 23:1).

26. Consecrated Obedience: Sharing Christ's Filial Relationship with the Father

In speaking about the obedient Christ and in asking for the grace to be conformed to the obedient Christ, we are opening ourselves wide up to being *a sign of contradiction in the world.* That is what Jesus was, and he was this sign of contradiction in a supreme way as he gave his life in obedience to his Father's will. *By his poverty Jesus enriched us; by his obedience he redeemed the world.*

In reflecting on religious obedience, various important aspects of this topic merit attention. Obedience is placed on *the highest possible level of relevance* in the spiritual life of Religious—sharing in Christ's filial relationship with his Father. How important it is to share in Christ's relationship with the Father and in his mission of salvation.

At this point it is useful to speak about *what Jesus accomplished by obedience* and *what obedience meant in his own life*—in his intimate relationship with the Father. *Christ brought humanity back to the Father by his obedience,* and every Christian must be united to this obedience and share in it in order to attain to God. All the more must Religious imitate Christ's obedience.

Total Love of the Father

In his own humanity Jesus is constituted Lord in his glorious resurrection, precisely because of his perfect obedience. Saint Paul reminds us that Christ "humbled himself, / becoming obedient to death, / even the death on a cross. / Because of this, God greatly exalted him / and bestowed on him the name / that is above every name, / that at the name of Jesus / every knee should bend... / and every tongue confess that / Jesus Christ is Lord, / to the glory of the Father" (Phil 2:8–11). How supremely important obedience was for Jesus! It was *the expression of his total love for the Father*. His human life began with the sentiments recorded in the Letter to the Hebrews: "then I said, '...Behold, I come to do your will, O God'" (Heb 10:7). The incarnation itself is the will of the Father and the incarnation takes Jesus to Calvary.

But before going to Calvary Jesus insists that it is to show his loving obedience to the Father. We remember those beautiful words that he speaks to us in the Gospel of St. John: "...the world must know that I love the Father and that I do just as the Father has commanded me. Get up, let us go" (John 14:31). At the moment of the culmination and consummation of his sacrifice on Calvary, Jesus spoke once again words of loving obedience to his Father: "Father, into your hands I commend my spirit" (Luke 23:46).

What then did this obedience mean for Jesus? *Love, total love*! But it was a love that passed through renunciation, resignation and suffering. Jesus had said: "Father not my will but thine be done."

Imitating Jesus

But why obedience on our part? To imitate Jesus. To share in his filial relationship with the Father. To share in his salvific activity. What does this mean? To live with Jesus for the Father. Jesus says: "I always do what is pleasing to him" (John 8:29). But how do we live for the Father? Here we have the great secret of the transfiguration when the voice of the heavenly Father was heard as Jesus was transfigured before his three special companions Peter, James and John. The Father said: "This is my beloved Son. Listen to him" (Mark 9:7). In virtue of the Father's command we are asked to give total acceptance to Jesus. We are asked to accept him in his identity. Here we are speaking of *the obedience of faith*, which includes the acceptance of his church, the acceptance of his sacraments, the acceptance of his word and his commandments.

And, yes, we are speaking about accepting that special evangelical counsel of supernatural obedience, *exercised within an approved institute of the church*, according to approved constitutions, in the context of a supernatural attitude of surrendering one's own will to the church, to Christ and to his Father. Here too there are discernments to be made on the part of superiors and on the part of each member of the community. Obedience is not passivity. Authority is not the capricious or arbitrary exercise of power. Neither authority nor obedience is pragmatic. Each is a charism, an ecclesial charism. In particular, obedience is a charism that springs from love and consummates love in sacrifice, in renunciation, in the oblation of the will, in the passion and cross of our Lord Jesus Christ.

It is because of the cross of Jesus and the sacrifice that he offered on the cross that we are able to understand and to live obedience—supernatural obedience—in the church. We remember the words of St. Cyril of Jerusalem, who says: "The Catholic Church glories in all Christ's actions, but her greatest glory is the Cross" (*Catechesis*, 13).

Obedience: Always Ecclesial

There are different forms of obedience in the church. The church wills that this obedience be determined in the approved constitutions of different congregations, but obedience is *always ecclesial*. It always embraces *the teaching of the church* and always is subject to *the Holy Father as the vicar of Christ*.

Certainly, at times, there may be questioning, but the response of obedience must always remain joyful even if, at the same time, it is demanding. Obedience is directed to Jesus Christ and his church and, with Jesus Christ, to his Father: "Not my will, but thine be done."

In the concrete, what does this obedience mean for Religious, by reason of their vow? It means, first of all, a fuller obedience to the church and to the Holy Father. *The Holy Father is your highest superior*. Obedience means respect for and obedience to the local bishop. It means acceptance of your constitutions and the willingness to be directed in your assignments and your apostolate by your superiors who have a special role of coordination. It also means in many ways consistent with your constitutions to give up your own will in given circumstances. In all of this, *the motivation is to be like Christ* and contribute supernaturally to the life of the church, *being conformed to Jesus in his life of renunciation*. In speaking about poverty, I already mentioned that the world would never tell you to be poor. Even more so, the world will never tell you to be obedient. Obedience is linked to the cross. Saint Paul tells us: "The message of the cross is foolishness to those who are perishing, but to us who are being saved it is the power of God" (1 Cor 1:18). Saint Paul then goes on to explain that: "It was the will of God through the foolishness of the proclamation to save those who have faith . . . but we proclaim Christ crucified, a stumbling block to Jews and foolishness to Gentiles, but to those who are called, Jews and Greeks alike, Christ the power of God and the wisdom of God. For the foolishness of God is wiser than human wisdom, and the weakness of God is stronger than human strength" (vv. 21–25).

The crucified Christ of whom St. Paul speaks is the obedient Christ. Through obedience, the church of Christ and, in particular, those in consecrated life participate in the cross and therefore in the foolishness of the gospel! The charism of obedience is linked with the hidden wisdom of the cross. In regard to obedience, your lives make sense not in the terms of the world but only to the extent that you can repeat the words of St. Paul: "For I resolved to know nothing while I was with you except Jesus Christ, and him crucified" (1 Cor 2:2).

The Christ who has called Religious to a life of obedience, and who shares with them in that obedience his filial relationship with the Father, will not abandon them in their desire to be faithful. They have every reason to say: *Jesus, I trust in you!*

27. Being, with Jesus, a Sign of Contradiction

There are many things to discuss with Jesus in a dialogue of love. Among these are his mission and yours.

Jesus shares with us the sentiments of his sacred heart regarding his own mission. He shares with us his enthusiasm and his anguish. He speaks to us about what is going to happen. He wants us *to enter into the thoughts of his heart.* Understanding him, we shall understand so much more about ourselves and what we are called to do in his name.

Jesus boldly states: "I have come to set the earth on fire, and how I wish it were already blazing!" (Luke 12:49). But he realizes—and he tells us—that his mission will cost him dearly. With those next words he is asking for our understanding and our consolation. He says: "There is a baptism with which I must be baptized, and how great is my anguish until it is accomplished!" (v. 50).

These words describe *the attitude of Jesus* in the face of his impending passion and death. Despite the anguish, he has an immense desire to be immersed— and this is the sense of his baptism—in the abyss of suffering that is necessary to lead him to the fulfillment of his mission.

The mission itself is to bring to the world the fire

of the Holy Spirit with all his purifying and renewing power.

In the gospel Jesus points out what is going to be the result of his action. He ratifies the prophecy that Simeon made about him when he was a child: he is to be "a sign of contradiction."

Jesus says it is true: "No, I tell you, but rather division" (v. 51)—the fundamental division between those who will accept him and those who will reject him. *All human liberty is challenged*: there are those who use it to accept Christ; there are those who use it to reject him.

Implicit in these words of Jesus is *the invitation to accept him and to accept his mission as our own*. He generously permits us to share in his work of bringing the fire of the Holy Spirit to the world. He reserves for us a share in his suffering and a share in his anguish. In effect, he is summoning us to walk forward with him and not to leave him until everything is accomplished. "What anguish I feel till it is over!"

Keeping Our Eyes Fixed on Jesus

Jesus has warned us that we cannot have it both ways. He is indeed the great sign of contradiction. If we follow him and his way of life, then we shall feel the burden of *being, with him, a sign of contradiction*. The world will pursue us relentlessly and mock us and tell us that we are benighted, "out of it," even reactionary. Any effort at appeasement on our part will be insufficient in the eyes of hostile opposition to the gospel. We have no choice but to admit that Jesus meant what he said when he said he came for division. And again he says: "Whoever is not with me is against me, and whoever who does not gather with me scatters" (Matt 12:30).

But how shall we face the challenge? The author of the Letter to the Hebrews lavishes encouragement on us (Heb 12:1–3). He wants us to picture ourselves in a stadium. There are many people watching us: "We are surrounded," he says, "by so great a cloud of witnesses." He gives the advice: we have to "rid ourselves of every burden and sin that clings to us and persevere in running the race that lies before us." Then come those words that tell us exactly what to do: "Let us keep our eyes fixed on Jesus, who inspires and perfects our faith." There follows a final exhortation: "Do not grow despondent or abandon the struggle." All of this presupposes that *God is with us* and will help us, and the church assures us that he will never leave us. Hence, our response: *Jesus, I trust in you!*

Surely we are challenged in the Christian life by great opposition. We shall have our share of temptations to yield, to give in. We shall need fortitude to fight cowardice. Was this not the temptation, described in the Book of the Prophet Jeremiah, to which King Zedekiah succumbed when, speaking of the innocent Jeremiah, he told the princes: "He is in your power." The cowardice could never be justified even though later on Zedekiah intervened to rescue Jeremiah from the cistern (cf. chap. 38).

In the face of Christian trials we ask on our part for wisdom and fortitude, serenity and joy to follow the Jesus, who is the sign of contradiction and who has bequeathed this role to his holy church and to all of us who have the privilege of being members of this holy church.

28. The New Millennium: The Word Became Flesh

Our Pilgrimage Continues

Ever since his election to the papacy, Pope John Paul II has been speaking to the church about *the great Jubilee of the year 2000*, the celebration of the millennium. He has presented the millennium as *the greatest anniversary in the history of the world*: the two-thousandth anniversary of the incarnation. Over and over again the Holy Father called it a wonderful opportunity for us to renew our fidelity to Jesus Christ.

At the beginning of the Jubilee Year, the Holy Father opened the holy door of St. Peter's Basilica with great hope. When he closed the holy door on the Feast of the Epiphany 2001, and joyfully recalled the legacy of the Great Jubilee, he noted that *the living door*, Jesus Christ, whom the holy door symbolizes *remains open*! As we have already entered the new millennium, perhaps we are better able now to share the Holy Father's vision in its totality. We are better able to reflect on the graces that we received during the three years of preparation and see where Christ leads us on our continuing pilgrimage.

The Holy Father has stated that the aim of the Jubilee and of its preparation was to recall and reawaken in us, an awareness of the key truth of faith, which St. John expressed at the beginning of his Gospel: "The Word became flesh / and made his dwelling among us" (John 1:14).

For the church the whole celebration of the new millennium is meaningful only in the light of the mystery of the incarnation and of its divine motivation and purpose. These are explained to us by St. John when he says: "God so loved the world that he gave his only Son, so that everyone who believes in him might not perish but might have eternal life" (John 3:16).

The pope constantly urged the church to be ready for this great event. He has also made a special appeal to the Religious of the church. In the address that he gave to the bishops of Region IX on June 13 of 1998, the Holy Father stated the following: "At the approach of the new Millennium, the Church urgently needs a vital and appealing religious life that shows forth concretely the sovereignty of God and bears witness before the world to the transcendent value of the 'total gift of self in the profession of the evangelical counsels'...."

Total Concentration on Jesus Christ

You can see how much Pope John Paul II was thinking about Religious in the church, how much he is counting on their help to make the Jubilee and the new millennium the spiritual celebration that it is meant to be, to draw the attention of the world to

Christ. In another place Pope John Paul II described the church's program for the millennium and its preparation. He said so beautifully that this program "must be *a total concentration on Jesus Christ*" (*Ad Limina* address to U.S. bishops, April 17, 1988). This is indeed what we were asked to accomplish.

In all our reflections it is not our intention to concentrate on ourselves but rather on Christ and on the mercy of God. The hour has come in the life of the church for us to express our total trust in Jesus Christ. We are all invited to say over and over again: *Jesus, I trust in you!*

Back in 1983 during the Holy Year of the Redemption the Holy Father issued a special call to conversion to all the members of the church, particularly to the Religious. We can see that the Holy Father once again counts on the Religious of the church to help make the third millennium what it is meant to be, a total concentration on Jesus Christ.

I wish to emphasize that the aim of the Jubilee was to reawaken in us an awareness of the incarnation and its consequences in our lives. The Holy Father is telling us that the church must proclaim Jesus Christ as victorious in the redemption that he brought about in his blood. We have reflected so often on the fact that the church's proclamation must begin with witness and personal testimony. Hence in the lives of Religious the church's proclamation in the millennium must be the proclamation of victory over sin and death accomplished by the one who is "the first-born of the dead" (Rev 1:5).

In the above-mentioned *Ad Limina* address, Pope John Paul II clearly presents to us the Christ of the millennium, telling us that he is "this firstborn from the dead, 'the king of kings and lord of lords' (Rev 19:16), the eternal Son of God, *the Word of God made flesh*, the person who identifies himself as 'the one who lives' (Rev 1:18) and who tells his Church 'there is nothing to fear' (v. 17).... The Christ of the Millennium is *the divine Christ of the Gospels* who has entered into his glory and who is forever alive in his word and in his Church. He is not a weak and ineffective Christ but a Christ who has triumphed throughout twenty centuries and who remains 'the power of God and the wisdom of God' (1 Cor 1:24)."

Vast Internal Renewal

We can see how very much alive the Christ of the millennium continues to be for the church. This Christ invites us to receive the Holy Spirit in our hearts and to be open to his action. We are invited to be part of *the vast internal renewal of the church*. We are invited to share in the new Pentecost. We are invited to put on, to assume new attitudes of humility, generosity and openness to the purifying action of the Holy Spirit. The Holy Father has said that the church of the millennium "must show that she is *vitally concerned with being faithful to Christ*; hence she must strive mightily to respond to the great challenges of holiness, evangelization and service" (*ibid.*).

189

Pope John Paul II also wanted us to know that the celebration of the Jubilee year was held in continuity with the Jubilee celebrations in the Old Testament. The church has assumed many of the aspects of the Jubilee from the Old Testament where it was meant to restore social justice, to protect the weak, to restore equality among people. The Holy Father presented the Jubilee as being "the year of the Lord's favor." He calls it "a year of the remission of sins and of the punishments due to them, a year of reconciliation between disputing parties, a year of manifold conversions and of sacramental and extra-sacramental penance" (*Tertio Millennio Adveniente*, 14).

The Holy Father made a particular point in telling us that the holy year was intended to be not only a year of joy but *a year of jubilation*. We were celebrating the incarnation of God's Son and hence, to the extent possible, the unity of all Christians. The Holy Father continues to challenge us to promote through prayer and holiness of life the unity of the church.

This brings us back to the agenda for the church that was expressed so authoritatively by the Second Vatican Council. Pope John Paul II has linked in a very intimate way the celebration of *the millennium to the Second Vatican Council*. He has stated: "The best preparation for the new Millennium, therefore, can only be expressed in a renewed commitment *to apply*, as faithfully as possible, *the teachings of Vatican II to the life of every individual and of the whole Church*" (*ibid.*, 20).

It is not surprising that the Holy Father vigorously called for an emphasis on evangelization during the whole millennium. He asked all the members of the church to be mindful of past sins, errors and instances of infidelity, inconsistency and slowness to act in corresponding to the demands of the gospel. He was confident that the acknowledgement and confession of sins would bring a greater commitment to the future of the church—a commitment to combat all forms of injustice. Once again the concentration of the millennium was not on sin, but rather on *the forgiveness of sins* and *the joy of conversion*—the conversion that leads us to new commitment and to fresh beginnings. The millennium was undoubtedly a call to conversion, holiness and life.

A great emphasis of the Jubilee was prayer. It is essential for the Holy Father that the church associate herself in prayer with Mary the Mother of Jesus, and that she rely on the power of the Holy Spirit to fulfill the ever more urgent mission of proclaiming the gospel of Christ to all the world. It is important for all the members of the church once again to find companionship with Jesus, to be with Jesus in order to be sent forth on the mission that is always pressing on the church.

Communion of the Most Blessed Trinity

As the Holy Father draws our attention to Jesus Christ, he does so by emphasizing Christ in the communion of the Most Blessed Trinity of which Christ is the second person. In a detailed way the Holy Father has told the church how to celebrate the mys-

tery of the Most Blessed Trinity always in union with
Jesus Christ her Lord. It is inspiring to recall how the
Holy Father divided the three years of immediate
preparation into three years honoring each individual person of the Most Blessed Trinity, always in the
context of the Trinity.

In 1997 the church celebrated the year of Jesus
Christ. We began our immediate journey to the
Father together with him who is the Son of God, the
Eternal Word Incarnate. It was the year to celebrate
our faith, to draw attention to the Bible, to emphasize the sacrament of baptism that is the sacrament of
faith, of divine adoption and of Christian initiation.
It was the year in which we drew attention to the
divine motherhood of our Blessed Mother.

In 1998, the Holy Father drew our attention to
the Holy Spirit, the third person of the Most Blessed
Trinity. It was the year that we celebrated the great
works of the Holy Spirit in the sacrament of confir-
mation. It was the year in which we acknowledged
the Holy Spirit as the one who builds the kingdom of
God, He is the one who inspires and sustains all
evangelization. In the Holy Spirit we can better
understand the many signs of hope that exist in the
church. In the Holy Spirit we can understand better
the Son whom St. Paul calls "Christ Jesus our hope"
(1 Tim 1:1). In the Holy Spirit we are committed to
the unity of the church, as we make our pilgrim way
to the Father, in the company of the woman Mary
who was so docile to the Holy Spirit.

The year 1999 was meant to lead us to the Father.
It is through the journey that we have undertaken

with Jesus himself, it is in the Holy Spirit that we make our pilgrimage to the house of the Father. This pilgrimage was a conversion journey in which the church made a massive effort to emphasize the sacrament of penance, the sacrament of the mercy of God. It was the year in which the third great theological virtue, charity, was emphasized throughout the church. It was the year in which we proclaimed our Blessed Mother Mary as the highly favored daughter of the Father. We can see how important that year was. It is Jesus himself, whom we have mentioned as being *Totus ad Patrem* (the one whose existence is totally directed to the Father), who leads us personally to his Father. After two thousand years he presents his beloved church to his beloved Father. This is the church for which he came into the world. This is the church that extends the principle of his own incarnation. This is the church for which he lived and died, the church that he loves and the church that he desires to see united with him in glory for all eternity.

Then came the moment when Christ presented this beloved church to his heavenly Father through the ministry of the pope. We have to realize that the last moment of preparation for the Jubilee Year 2000 was a moment of exultation for Christ himself. In the gospels we find him exulting in the Holy Spirit, and now once again he exults in the Holy Spirit as he offers the trophy of his own blood, his beloved church, purified through his own death and resurrection, to his Father.

The year 2000 celebrated the mystery of the Most Blessed Trinity: Father, Son and Holy Spirit. The church acknowledges the mystery of God's life, one in three and three in one. All her efforts during that year drew attention to the most blessed sacrament, to the Eucharist, for it is through the Eucharist that the church will be able to participate in the death and resurrection of the Son of God and hence be admitted into communion with the Most Blessed Trinity forever. The year 2000 was the year of supreme jubilation as the church purified and converted renewed her own commitment to continue on the way until the final phase in the Father's house.

Back in 1988 the Holy Father already foresaw the final phase of the millennium celebration. He stated: "Presiding over every celebration of the Millennium will be the Eucharistic Lord himself, renewing his Church and presenting her to the Father in union with himself. It is mainly through the Eucharist that the Millennium will actuate the power of the redemption. In the Eucharist the Church will find the sure source and guarantee of her commitment to the service of humanity" (Address of April 17, 1988).

Why do we still emphasize the millennium? Because the beginning of the new millennium is just that: a new beginning. It is not a moment in time after which we "return to ordinary routine!" It energizes and inspires us to continue our lifelong pilgrimage. It was such an important part of our life, such a significant moment in the life of the church, and we belong to the church! Our individual journey to the Father, our journey together in the new millennium must continue to pass through the eucharistic celebration into the heart of Jesus and through that heart into the communion of the Most Blessed Trinity.

29. The Assumption of Mary: A Sign of Sure Hope

On the solemnity of the Assumption of our Blessed Mother the whole church expresses immense joy by addressing Mary in the words of the Hail Mary: "Blessed art thou among women, and blessed is the fruit of thy womb, Jesus." These are the words of Elizabeth, to which the church has added the holy name of Jesus, the name that Mary and Joseph gave to the child, acting on instructions from the angel.

We proclaim the defined faith of the church: that after her earthly life, *Mary was taken up, body and soul, into heavenly glory*. This was the solemn proclamation of Pope Pius XII on November 1, 1950. But even more, this is what the church has taught and lived for all the centuries.

We stop to reflect on what we hold and proclaim by faith. How magnificent is God's plan for his Mother! How magnificent is God's plan for his church, of which his Mother is the type and exemplar!

Saint Paul proclaims: "Christ has been raised from the dead," adding that he is, "the firstfruits of those who have fallen asleep" (1 Cor 15:20). The church knows how to explain to us the mystery of Mary's assumption. She does this by recalling to us that Christ is the firstfruits; Mary, the second.

We believe that Mary fell asleep in death. In this she was like her Son Jesus. But she was then assumed body and soul into heavenly glory. In Mary's life the assumption is not only the event parallel to Christ's ascension; it is also the event parallel to Christ's resurrection.

The church honors Mary as the Mother of Jesus, the Mother of God. She gave the Eternal Word his flesh, his sacred humanity. She nurtured him. She was with him when he died. And then the glory that he experienced in his flesh at the time of his resurrection, Christ reserved to his Mother to share also. By the power of his own resurrection, Jesus communicated life to his Mother and then assumed her to be with himself and his Father and the Holy Spirit in heavenly glory.

The church kneels in profound admiration of God's revealed plan for Mary. The church proclaims, in human terms, how fitting it is that the flesh of Mary that gave flesh to the Son of God should never know corruption.

Body and Soul in Heavenly Glory

Saint Paul goes further. He speaks to us about *our* future resurrection: "Christ the firstfruits; then, at his coming, those who belong to Christ" (1 Cor 15:23). We shall have to wait our turn. But meanwhile, Mary goes before us, in the words of the Second Vatican Council, as "a sign of sure hope." It is especially in her assumption that Mary shows herself to be this sign of sure hope for the whole church, to which she is so intimately related as Mother.

The Book of Revelation speaks of the woman. In this woman, Mary is seen in her relationship to the church. But the Book of Revelation speaks about the woman wailing aloud in pain as she labored to give birth. We are convinced, however, that the birth of Jesus was a special birth without the pains of labor. It is rather in the second act of maternity—bringing forth the church—that Mary experiences pain and labor and deep suffering at the foot of the cross.

We honor Mary as Mother of the church. And what happened to her will happen to each of us in due time. Although we must wait, we believe in the glorification of our body and soul together in heaven. *First* Christ, *then* Mary, *then* the entire church, or as Saint Paul says: "all those who belong to him."

The late Cardinal Timothy Manning, archbishop of Los Angeles, used to make a beautiful comment in reference to the assumption. He was convinced that in the history of the church there are two reasons for the solemn definition of a dogma by the pope. One is its denial; another reason is the appropriateness of the teaching to a particular age. Cardinal Manning mentioned that in 1950 the church's teaching on the assumption was not denied. It was, however, the moment for the church to proclaim the sacredness of the human body. The concentration camps like Auschwitz and Buchenwald had consummated nationalism and cremated liberty. Human flesh had seemingly no value, no sacredness. At this juncture in history the church responded by showing what God thinks of human flesh: it is *worthy of eternal glory and of union with the Most Blessed Trinity*. Not only does Jesus the

Son of God bring his human flesh to heaven, but he wills that his Mother Mary should be with him, in her body and soul.

The two of them, Jesus and Mary together, await all the sons and daughters of Mary, the brothers and sisters of Jesus who, professing the resurrection of Jesus and the assumption of Mary, are themselves being prepared for the day of eternal glory.

Mary, in your assumption, all generations call you blessed! And all generations will see in your assumption that the trust you had in Jesus is totally justified. As we await the day of our own heavenly glory we imitate your trust and, with you, say to Jesus: *Jesus, I trust in you!*"

30. *The Holy Spirit: Love of the Father and the Son*

It is always a great joy to proclaim the mystery of God's life: that God is a Father, that Christ is the Son of his eternal love, that the Holy Spirit is the third person, the personal love whereby the Father and the Son love each other eternally.

From all eternity we know that God lives in the communion of three divine persons. Because of his love, God wishes to share his divine life. We often speak of God as Creator, Redeemer and Sanctifier. We know that all God's actions in the world are common to the three divine persons. None of the three divine persons is isolated in creating, redeeming and sanctifying. And yet the church often "attributes" one or other action of God to one or other person of the Most Blessed Trinity. We know that the three divine persons are distinct. The places they occupy in the Trinity are distinct, one from another. Still, *some actions that God performs in relation to the world bear a likeness, humanly speaking, to the role that belongs particularly to one of the divine persons.*

Completion and Perfection "Attributed" to the Holy Spirit

We know that the Holy Spirit, as the love of the Father and the Son, completes the term of the divine operations and brings to conclusion the cycle of the divine life. Hence, whatever is a work of completion and perfection, a work of holiness and love is "attributed" to the Holy Spirit. In this way the church expresses her faith, proclaiming the life of the Most Blessed Trinity and the place that the third person holds in the communion of God's intimate life. The delicate work of sanctification is thus attributed to the Holy Spirit, who is known as "the finger of God's right hand"—*digitus paternae dexterae*.

Not only does the church use this form of "attributing" an external work of God to one person in the Most Blessed Trinity, but this form is also found in the scriptures. It is likewise used by Jesus himself.

The Holy Spirit then in the church, as the love of the Father and the Son—love that is identical with life in the Trinity—is called *the giver of life*. The Holy Spirit is also looked upon as the *supreme source of unity* in the church—unity which is a gift of perfection in the community of Christ's disciples. The Holy Spirit is also called by Jesus the *counselor* of the apostles. It is he who guarantees that the teaching of Jesus will be understood. It is he who actually bears witness to Jesus in the world. From the entire life of the church we know that the reason Jesus sent the Holy

Spirit is *that the Holy Spirit may form Jesus in us.* His role in the church is *to enable us to participate in the filial relationship of Jesus to the Father,* or in other words to become the children of God. Saint Paul tells us: "Those who are led by the Spirit of God are children of God" (Rom 8:14).

"Person-Love"—"Person-Gift"

In his encyclical letter *Dominum et Vivificantem,* the Holy Father speaks of the Holy Spirit, calling him "Person—Love" and again "Person—Gift." The Holy Spirit is indeed the third person of the Most Blessed Trinity. His identity is love. His personhood is love. It is most accurate to describe him as "Person —Love." At the same time the Holy Spirit who proceeds from the Father and the Son is sent into the world and given to the world as a gift.

In the Gospel of St. John we read that the Father gives the Holy Spirit (cf. John 14:16). And we read again that the Father sends the Holy Spirit in the name of the Son (cf. John 4:26), and that the Spirit bears witness to the Son (cf. John 15:26), and we likewise read that the Son asks the Father to send the Holy Spirit and at the same time Jesus speaks of himself sending the Holy Spirit: "If I go, I will send him to you" (John 16:7). We see therefore that the Father sends the Holy Spirit in the power of his Fatherhood, just as he has sent the Son. And at the same time he sends him in the power of the redemption accomplished by Christ. And in this sense the

Holy Spirit is sent also by the Son. And so we can see how accurate it is to describe the Holy Spirit not only as "Person—Love" but also as "Person—Gift": the great gift that is given to the church by the Father and the Son.

Jesus made a point of telling the apostles that it was advantageous for them that he should go away, in other words that he should return to the Father. His departure was the condition for the coming of the Holy Spirit upon the church at Pentecost (cf. John 16:7).

Jesus offers the Holy Spirit to the church to dwell in the church and to confirm the church in her identification with Jesus. And so the gift, the "Person—Gift," that Jesus sends, together with his Father, remains in the church for all generations *to direct the activity of the church* and to help the church fulfill her mission of sanctification in the world. The proclamation of the gospel—the whole work of evangelization—all throughout the centuries will be directed by the Holy Spirit as "the finger of God's right hand." Already in the Acts of the Apostles we see the history of the early church as being the history of the intervention of the Holy Spirit in the world.

The Principal Evangelizer

Our mission today of evangelization, our activities of catechetics are all under the sovereign direction of the Holy Spirit. The Holy Spirit is the principal evangelizer. Jesus acting in the power of the Holy

Spirit evangelizes, catechizes and teaches through us; everything that is done in the name of Jesus is done through the power of the Holy Spirit. The Letter to the Hebrews will say that Jesus "through the eternal spirit offered himself unblemished to God" (Heb 9:14) in sacrifice on the cross through the power of the Spirit.

At this point it is very important to insist on the role of *the Holy Spirit in evangelization* in all its spheres, especially that of catechetics. Let us listen to some very important words of Pope Paul VI. They spell out at length the action of the Holy Spirit. The Holy Father states: "It must be said that the Holy Spirit is the principal agent in evangelization: it is he who impels each individual to proclaim the Gospel, and it is he who in the depths of consciences causes the word of salvation to be accepted and understood." We must continue to listen to this deep reflection because it is very relevant for our lives. It is very relevant for all our teaching activity in the church. Pope Paul VI goes on: "The Holy Spirit is the soul of the Church. It is he who explains to the faithful the deep meaning of the teaching of Jesus and of his mystery. It is the Holy Spirit who, today just as at the beginning of the Church, acts in every evangelizer who allows himself to be possessed and led by him. The Holy Spirit places on his lips the words which he could not find by himself, and at the same time the Holy Spirit predisposes the soul of the hearer to be open and receptive to the good news and to the kingdom being proclaimed." Pope Paul VI then brings us to a level of sobering realism and demanding humility by adding: "Techniques of evangelization are good but even the most advanced ones could not replace the gentle action of the Spirit. The most perfect preparation of the evangelizer has no effect without the Holy Spirit. Without the Holy Spirit the most convincing dialectic has no power over the heart of man. Without him the most highly developed schemes resting on a sociological or psychological basis are quickly seen to be quite valueless.... It is not by chance that the great inauguration of evangelization took place on the morning of Pentecost under the inspiration of the Spirit" (*Evangelii Nuntiandi*, 75).

Giver of Freedom

As we look to the Holy Spirit, we see that we must prayerfully reflect on *his role in the Most Blessed Trinity*, on *the impact that the Holy Spirit had on Christ*, on *His activity in the church*, and *in our own souls*. I leave it to you to recall the various gifts of the Holy Spirit as they are contained in the *Catechism of the Catholic Church*. The sevenfold gifts of the Holy Spirit are indeed relevant to our lives as baptized and confirmed Christians and so very much a part of consecrated life. But one gift in particular that I would like to emphasize today is *freedom*. The Holy Spirit is the giver of true freedom.

You know that the more you reflect the more you see that the world wants to enslave you. It wants to enslave you with falsehood, with aberrant theories, with nontruthful fads and in many other ways that will yoke you under bonds that are not worthy of the New Testament of Christ. There are theories and practices; there are many things that are proposed as fact that simply are not true. One example with many consequences for Christian freedom and for truth is the question of *what constitutes* "exclusive language." Language that is truly exclusive and therefore truly unjust cannot be language that has simply been declared such by someone who is promoting his or her own agenda. There are many areas where it is necessary in the church today to reaffirm not only the truth of Christianity but the freedom for which Christ set us free (cf. Gal 5:1). And it is the Holy Spirit who reminds us of our freedom and confirms us in the gift of this freedom. Saint Paul tells us that "where the Spirit of the Lord is, there is freedom" (2 Cor 3:17).

"The Forgiveness of Sin"

The Holy Spirit has different titles, some from sacred scripture, some from the piety of the church. One of the titles by which the church refers to him is "the forgiveness of sins" (*Ipse est remissio peccatorum*).

What a special joy it is to proclaim *that the forgiveness of sins is attributed to the Holy Spirit* in the church. Indeed, this act of God's mercy is identified with his love and therefore with the Holy Spirit. For this reason the church can call the Holy Spirit "the forgiveness of sins."

We are called frequently to meditate on sin, but only in order *to proclaim God's mercy and forgiveness.* In honoring the Holy Spirit we proclaim that *he is indeed the forgiveness of sins.* The divine action of pardon or forgiveness is identified with his nature and attributed to his person. Through the action of the Holy Sprit, we are able to proclaim that "where sin increased, grace overflowed all the more" (Rom 5: 20). All the infidelity of God's people, all the sins of the world are *nothing compared with the merciful forgiveness of God,* made possible by the death of Jesus Christ who offered himself in the power of the Holy Spirit, who is God's Love. When Jesus gave the apostles the power to forgive sins, he first communicated to them the Holy Spirit saying: "Receive the holy Spirit. Whose sins you forgive are forgiven them, and whose sins you retain are retained" (John 20:22–23). What great confidence Jesus deserves for giving us the Holy Spirit to keep alive forgiveness in the church! He deserves our response: *Jesus, I trust in you!*

And, honoring the Holy Spirit we proclaim the forgiveness of sins and the power of God's Love to conquer them: all of our sins and the sins of the whole world.

Consecration to the Holy Spirit

We also proclaim *the power of the Holy Spirit to form Jesus* ever more in each of us, and then to sustain us in Christian living and in all the ideals of

Christian discipleship and of the various particular vocations.

In the gospel the young man is challenged by Jesus with a radical invitation. It is this: "Go, sell...give ...come, follow me" (Matt 19:21). The gospel said that the young man was not up to the invitation: "He went away sad." You, dear friends, have accepted the invitation joyfully and are running the course. *Perseverance is a great gift of the Holy Spirit.* Today we proclaim his power to sustain us to the end!

In speaking about the Holy Spirit, I frequently evoke the memory of Pope Leo XIII. In the year 1897 Pope Leo wrote his famous encyclical on the Holy Spirit, called *Divinum Illud.* He was eighty-seven at the time and perceived that he was approaching death. Actually, he lived for another six years and died in 1903 at the age of ninety-three. But what was so important for Pope Leo was his action *to consecrate to the Holy Spirit all the work of his long pontificate.* In consecrating his service as pope to the Holy Spirit, he prayed that the Holy Spirit would bring his work to fruitfulness and completion.

His was an *act of piety* toward the Holy Spirit, but also *an act of faith* in the doctrine of the Most Blessed Trinity. By "attributing" to the Holy Spirit whatever is a work of loving completion, we do not exclude the action of the Father and the Son. By no means. But we do recognize, by what the church calls "attribution," the role that is peculiarly personal to the Holy Spirit. We proclaim the faith of the church that teaches that in the Most Blessed Trinity the Holy

Spirit is indeed the term of the divine operations. The Father loves the Son and the Son loves the Father, and the Holy Spirit is the expression of their love. In his person *the Holy Spirit brings to completion and perfection the cycle of the divine life.* In her prayer the church professes this mystery of God's trinitarian life and "attributes" to the Holy Spirit a work which, while common to the Holy Trinity, expresses a relationship to the role that belongs exclusively to the Holy Spirit within the communion of the Most Blessed Trinity.

As Pope Leo did, as the church does, so we too today invoke the Holy Spirit and proclaim his role in the communion of the three divine persons. In order to show this faith we consecrate to him our activities and our life so that he will bring them to the perfection of love—which he is in the Most Blessed Trinity!

We ask the Holy Spirit *to consummate us in his love.* He is the Spirit of holiness who engenders holiness in us. He is the Spirit who intercedes for us, and confirms us in the power to pray and to be the instruments of his intercession. As the Spirit of Jesus, he is the one that inculcates trust in us, the one who enables us to pronounce the holy name of Jesus, the one who enables us to proclaim our trust in Jesus, the one who makes it possible for us to say: "Jesus is Lord!" and *Jesus, I trust in you!*

We acknowledge that the Holy Spirit can do all this, and we invoke him with our pentecostal prayer: Come Holy Spirit, fill the hearts of your faithful and kindle in them the fire of your love:

Wash what is unclean;
Water what is arid;
Heal what is wounded.

Bend what is rigid;
Warm what is frigid;
Set straight what is crooked;
Give to your faithful
    who trust in you
      your seven holy gifts.

Give the reward of virtue;
Give a holy death;
Give eternal joy. Amen.